Lost Restaurants

of

SANTA CRUZ COUNTY

•••••••••••••••••••••••••••••••••••• LIZ POLLOCK

Liz Pollock

AMERICAN PALATE

Published by American Palate
A Division of The History Press
Charleston, SC
www.historypress.com

Front cover: Sāba Club and Caribbean Ballroom in Capitola, postcard. Sāba: "Named after a beautiful island in the Caribbean, the entrance is through an exotic atmosphere of authentic native spears, shields, dug-out canoes, flora and fauna." *Author's collection.*
Front cover: Chop Stick in Watsonville. Photograph dated 1972. *Courtesy of the Pajaro Valley Historical Association.*
Front cover: Ottaviano Chachie and staff, 1980s. Chachie's Hot Dogs, the classic choice for beachgoers. *Courtesy of the Seaside Company.*
Front cover: Pronto Pup, Watsonville. Advertisement in the 1958 Watsonville High School yearbook, Manzanita. *Courtesy of the Pajaro Valley Historical Association.*
Back cover: Postcard showing the courtyard and tables outside of the Cooper House, often referred to as the "Heart and Soul" of downtown Santa Cruz. *Author's collection.*
Back cover: "See You on the Beach at Santa Cruz." Matchbook. *Author's Collection.*
Back cover: Hodgie Wetzel working the order window at Hodgie's, 1980s. Hodgie Wetzel helped organize the Brussels Sprouts Festival at the Boardwalk in 1981. *Courtesy of the Seaside Company.*
Opposite page: Photograph of the author's husband, Steve Pollock, in 1985. *Author's collection.*

First published 2020
Manufactured in the United States

ISBN 9781467143851

Library of Congress Control Number: 2019954295

This book is dedicated to Gracie and Sammy Pollock and was written in loving memory of my husband, Steve Pollock.

Contents

CONTENTS

Acknowledgements

I would like to give many thanks to Leo Stefani, Dr. Paul A. Lee, Al McLean, Judy Steen, Joe Michalak, Rita Bottoms, Marion Dale Pokriots, Carolyn Swift, Christina Waters, Bruce McPherson, Sam Leask, Sheila O'Neil, Deborah Lipoma, Jay Topping, Susan Renison, Penny Castillo, Marla Novo and Jessie Durant. Special thanks to Gary Green and Christina Glynn of Visit Santa Cruz County for their support.

Most of the photographs and illustrations are from my own personal collection of menus, matchbooks and maps. I am grateful to Norman Davis, who loaned several unique historical pieces from his own extensive collection.

I would also like to thank Laurie Krill, my acquisitions editor at The History Press, for her guidance and encouragement.

Introduction

Millions of people come to Santa Cruz County to enjoy the Santa Cruz Beach Boardwalk, the beaches, the hotels and the restaurants. This book is about the history of the lost restaurants of Santa Cruz County and covers the fifty-year period between 1940 and 1990. The restaurants mentioned in this book were the unforgettable places where tourists and locals ordered cocktails, ate freshly caught seafood and rib-eye steaks and enjoyed authentic Italian cuisine with bottles of local California wine. My hope is that this book brings back good memories of dining at these restaurants while celebrating family reunions, wedding receptions and holiday parties.

When writing this book, I researched 194 restaurants that were family-owned and operated in Santa Cruz County (I avoided franchises and chains). The lifespan of these restaurants varied, depending on whether they survived World War II; the Korean War; the Vietnam War; the disastrous floods of 1955 and 1982; the incoming University of California (UCSC) campus in the mid-1960s and the hippie movement; the credit card and the computer revolution; and the major earthquake of 1989. I attempted to respectfully represent the many influential cultures of the area and showcased the many American, Italian, Mediterranean, Mexican, Indian, French, Polish, Hungarian, Swiss, Croatian, German, Greek, Armenian, Polynesian, Japanese, Filipino, Thai, Korean and Chinese restaurants. I also have included the places that specialized in Soul Food.

For this book, I interviewed seventy-eight people, and when gathered together, they form an oral history of restaurant workers and the many locals who enjoyed reminiscing about these places. I met with owners, managers, bartenders, waiters, waitresses, chefs and line cooks—everyone who helped create convivial atmospheres and serve great food. I also focused on the people behind the scenes who were in the business of serving the restaurants: the purveyors. I sat down with suppliers of linen; ice; wine and liquor; everyday equipment, like pots and pans; computers; bread; produce; and meat and seafood. I also spoke with the owners of the company that regularly services the restaurants' grease traps—because they are all members of the restaurant community. I enjoyed listening to them describe how and why they got into the restaurant business—what fueled their passion. Often, during an interview, I could see that talking brought back memories of certain people and special mentors, people who influenced their work ethic, technique, standards and outlook on the world. Many described their former bosses or fellow employees ("Oh, he was such a character!") and places long gone ("They used to have terrific food.").

After college, I went to the American Bartenders School in San Jose and became a Certified Mixologist. I was later hired at Adolph's Italian Family Style Restaurant as their first female bartender, and I worked a combination of the day and night shifts from 1985 to 1990. While working there, I met my husband and made many good friends.

The restaurant and hotel bars in Santa Cruz County naturally adapted to the times and sought to serve both the new and the old-fashioned cocktails. While conducting research for this book, I looked for a drink's popularity and whether it became popular through the efforts of the restaurant manager or a promotion by a liquor distributor. I've always been curious about cocktail history; I collect cocktail menus, bartender manuals and instruction booklets, some dating back to the early 1880s. Reading back issues of bartending trade magazines also gave me a great deal of information. I chose to include the recipes of fifteen cocktails—three for each decade—that I saw listed most often in menus from each period and which I know were most often requested by patrons during those years. I have also included notes and stories behind each of the recipes.

When looking over Santa Cruz County's broad range of cuisines and the nearly two hundred restaurants that have conducted business in the area for over fifty years, it is clear that this region has offered a rich variety of choices for a long time. I hope my readers will find that this book starts a conversation. There have been many restaurants in Santa Cruz County, and a complete collection of their names and menus would result in something like a giant encyclopedia. It is not my intention to exclude any restaurant, and there is no implication that a restaurant's omission from this book is a non-recommendation.

Chapter 1

The 1940s

RATION BOOKS AND RATIONING

In the 1940s, Santa Cruz County was an ideal place to grow up, and it was considered by many to be a retirement community. The 1940 Census for Santa Cruz County listed that the region's population was 45,057. Tourists traveling with their families would come to Santa Cruz to relax on the beach, sail, play golf and other sports, dine at unique restaurants and spend time at the Santa Cruz Beach Boardwalk. The main thoroughfares in Santa Cruz are Ocean Street, Pacific Avenue, Soquel Avenue, Mission Street and Beach Street. All are places where one could find a hotel and a general store for groceries, clothes, tools, hardware, souvenirs and more. The main routes to Santa Cruz were, and still are, Highway 17 from San Jose and Highway 1, which runs north to Davenport and south to Watsonville. Highway 9 goes up to Felton, Ben Lomond and Boulder Creek. During the 1940s, Santa Cruz County's main industries were agriculture, fishing and manufacturing.

Rationing and food shortages had huge impacts on average citizens and the restaurants in Santa Cruz County during the 1940s. The lives of restaurant owners and their employees were significantly changed and forever interrupted by World War II; many joined the service, while others remained at home and accepted jobs where their work was going toward the war effort. Several people who lived through these war years have shared their recollections of food rationing and ration books and describe the changes that were made to their everyday lives.

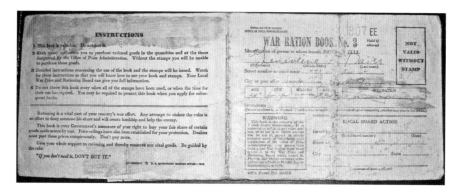

War ration book, 1943. Property of Genevieve Davis. *Courtesy of Norman Davis.*

Beginning on May 4, 1942, according to ration book guidelines, citizens lined up at elementary schools, ready to receive Ration Book 1; registration was from 2:00 p.m. to 9:00 p.m. Local elementary and secondary school teachers volunteered to handle the registration process. The *Santa Cruz Sentinel* reported on Friday, May 8, "A total of 35,608 ration books were issued according to County Rationing Administrator, Lloyd Bowman." Newspapers tried to help consumers by giving advice on how to use the new ration books; for example, they explained how one could make ration points go further. Grocery stores set up large displays and signage with some suggestions, for instance, "Take all the ration books in the family with you when you shop," (because family members' stamps could be used, even if they were not actually in the store).

Restaurant owners in Santa Cruz County, in addition to coping with food rations and the decrease in tourism, were officially required to maintain fair prices and to post this information on site.

The Office of Price Administration (OPA) imposed a strict policy for restaurant operators: they were to document the number of meals served during the month of December 1942. This number would then determine what the restaurant could charge as its "ceiling price" for the next year. But if these figures were considered too low or incorrect, the restaurant owner had to fill out a form explaining this discrepancy before petitioning the local rationing board for a price increase. In tourist towns like Santa Cruz, the sales data for December would naturally be different from the sales data in July, since summer months reflect the height of tourist season. Regardless, the OPA certifications were required to be posted in plain sight and printed on every revised menu. "All prices listed are at or below our

TO THE PROPRIETOR

You may not use this poster until you have filed your base period menus
or price lists with your Local War Price and Rationing Board.

Read the following carefully before you make any entries on this poster.

1. Study the list or lists of 40 basic food items which appear in the posting order issued by your OPA District Director. You must use the list which most nearly covers the kinds of foods you serve.

2. Have before you, your own copies of the menus or price lists which are the same as those that you filed with your Local War Price and Rationing Board in the past. Make out the list, in triplicate, of the items listed on your own menus or price list if those items appear on the District Director's list of 40 basic items. If you do not offer all of the items that appear on the District Director's list, write down as many as you do offer and then add to the list as many more of your own popular food items needed to make up the total of 40 items.

3. If you did not file your menus or price lists, you must do so immediately. Failure to file is a violation of the law and you are prohibited from using this poster until you have filed your menus or price lists.

4. Now, with the list of 40 items before you, write down your ceiling prices. Next, do the following (please do this carefully): If you had more than one price for the same item, that is one price for lunch, another price for dinner, and another for à la carte, write after the name of the item, which type of meal you are pricing. For instance: Steak dinner, or steak lunch, or steak à la carte.

5. Be sure to put in the correct price for coffee which will be 5¢ per cup, unless you have reported to your Board that you sold coffee for more than 5¢ in October 4–10, 1942.

6. If you customarily charged higher prices on Sundays, then be sure to print or write plainly at the top of your poster the following words: "These prices apply on week days only."

7. If you do not handle as many as 40 items, then fill in the poster with all of the items that you do offer.

8. After you have carefully made out your list of 40 items, in triplicate, fill in the 40 blank spaces on the poster with the same items, giving the name of the item, and stating whether the item is for lunch or dinner, if either is the case, and then inserting the prices. Please do this as neatly as possible, in clear large letters that can be seen 6 feet or more away. Your letters can be handwritten or printed. If they are printed, the letters must be ⅜ inch high and in solid bold-face type.

9. If you make a mistake in filling in the prices on the poster, do not make any erasures. In that case, get a new form from the OPA. It is unlawful to make any erasures or changes of prices on the poster.

10. Mail all three of your price lists to your Local War Price and Rationing Board. Be sure to write your name and address, signature of owner or manager, and date, clearly on each list. You may bring them to the Board in person, if you care to do so. As soon as possible, the War Price and Rationing Board will compare your price list with your filed menu prices and if it finds that there are no differences, one copy will be returned to you signed by the War Price and Rationing Board. That copy you must keep on your premises for inspection. If your price list does not agree with your filed prices, you will be notified by your War Price and Rationing Board to appear before it to correct your errors. In the case of corrections, it will be necessary for you to make out a new poster to conform to the facts.

The foregoing instructions are general and are offered for your convenience. You should thoroughly understand the complete Regulation which governs all of your prices.

Office of Price Administration (OPA) official form #6152–1036. "Any erasure or changes on this poster are unlawful." *Author's collection.*

ceiling prices. By OPA regulation, our ceiling prices are our highest prices from [date] to [date], 194[date]. Records of these prices are available for your inspection." Intact OPA posters that detail the rules for each restaurant owner are now quite rare.

Institutions, such as restaurants, hotels and hospitals, were instructed to apply for their ration books at the high schools. Restaurants were issued between 20 and 30 percent more ration coupons for sugar, flour, processed foods, canned goods and meat than private citizens. For restaurants, receiving more sugar, flour and meat was important because it meant they could continue making their signature dishes and baked goods. The length of time the coupons were valid changed every three to four months in order to prevent any counterfeiting. When new ration books were released, everyone went back to the OPA authority to officially sign up for new coupons; this was also when restaurant owners would restock their supplies. Naturally, the survival of Santa Cruz's restaurants was helped by the fact that citizens were allowed to use cash to pay for their meals, particularly if they ran out of coupons before the new ones were issued. During these frugal years, it helped a person's morale to go out—even if for a simple cup of coffee and a piece of pie—and be with neighbors and friends. Local restaurants were also very fortunate that the climate in Santa Cruz allowed them to find locally grown fruit and produce throughout the entire year.

Along with food rations, non-essential travel laws were also enforced, which curtailed tourism. Local car dealers went from selling new cars to selling used cars and promoting repair services. Tires were scarce, since rubber was needed in the war effort. The consumer received an "A" card, which allowed for just three gallons of gas per week. According to the "Occupational Driving Requirements," truck companies also had to fill out their own applications to receive more gas coupons than the private citizen. This had a big impact on the scheduling of regular deliveries of meat, produce, ice and eggs to restaurants and institutions. Trucking companies like these received "T" stickers to post on their trucks' windshields. Santa Cruz's local newspaper regularly warned about thieves and reported that ration books were often stolen out of glove compartments.

Registration for Ration Book 2 began on February 22, 1943, and Ration Book 3 was issued on May 28, 1943. Ration Book 4 introduced tokens, which went into effect in February 1944; tokens were considered to be beneficial because they never expired. In August 1945, the government stopped printing ration books altogether; however, sugar was rationed until 1947.

During this time, many women took on the responsibility of running their families' restaurants while their husbands, sons and uncles were serving in the military. Or they simply decided to close the restaurants temporarily, as Tea Cup co-owner Rose Yee did until her husband, Dan Y. Lee, came back from the army (he returned in 1946). Women were put in charge of managing ration coupons, ordering supplies, stocking groceries, keeping the accounts, paying bills, hiring new employees (if possible) and, in general, "making do." Restaurant owners had to repair old equipment, like gas ranges and range boilers, but any plans to upgrade to a newer model were put on hold until the war was over. In 1943, the *Spiegel Catalog* stated, "The sale of plumbing equipment, gas ranges and heating equipment, including gas, oil, coal and wood heaters, is restricted by government order." There was an itemized application that described emergency repairs. "[Emergency repairs are] necessary to maintain minimum heating and sanitary conditions required for public health. These remedial repairs are necessary because of imminent breakdown of plumbing or heating equipment which is worn out or damaged beyond repair." This meant if a repairman could not fix a damaged gas line or water pipe, the restaurant would have to explain why each repair was impractical and itemize the equipment that needed to be removed. These restrictions were accepted with phrases like, "We're making the best of the situation," and "We all have to manage until this war is over."

Restaurant menus also went through radical design changes during the rationing years. The Art Deco menu designs of the 1920s and 1930s, with fancy highlights of gold and glitter, were a thing of the past. In contrast, menus in the 1940s were printed on low-quality, inexpensive paper. (At the time, paper mills were completing war work assignments, and former mill workers and shop printers may have already been drafted.) According to local historian Judy Steen, "Polk's Santa Cruz Directories for 1942 to 1945 are missing, either because of self-imposed paper shortages or due to security reasons, because of its location, being a coastal city during World War II." During the war, printers used the same cheap pulp paper that was used for the mass printing of the Armed Services Editions of popular novels that were sent to the men and women in uniform. Menus had fewer pages; most often, they were just covers, with the entrée selections printed on the inside and a list of cocktails on the back. A patriotic quote of "Buy War Bonds" was sometimes printed on the inside corner. If there was a daily special, there was a small piece of paper that listed it—sometimes handwritten, and attached with a paperclip, straight pin or staple. Glossy and fancy outer covers were unavailable and unattainable during the war.

Due to a nationwide shortage of meat (most of it was going to the troops), the OPA declared that Tuesdays, along with Fridays, would be meatless. Since there was less meat, the restaurant menus may have listed lamb stew rather than lamb chops and beef stroganoff instead of a steak and promoted a variety of different vegetables. On June 30, 1943, the *Santa Cruz Sentinel* reported, "Meat Market Shelves Bare. At noon today, one Santa Cruz restaurant had a leg of lamb, another had chicken, one had beef and the remaining eateries were focusing their attention on appetizing fish and vegetable dinners." Menus stated that no substitutions were allowed, and margarine was served when butter became very scarce. Milk by the glass was restricted; it was only to be used for cooking. Ordering coffee at a restaurant meant just getting one cup; there were no seconds or top-offs, and customers could only add one teaspoon of sugar. The "help yourself" sugar bowls were taken off of tables; instead, waitresses would either have a teaspoon ready on their trays or they would offer sugar in a tiny single-serve dish. Restaurant employees also played a role in local scrap drives by rinsing and crushing tin cans and collecting grease to then turn in to the butcher. Due to a shortage of employees and the blackout periods at night, restaurants were open for fewer hours. Quoting from the popular 1944 travel guide by Duncan Hines, *Adventures in Good Eating*, "During these trying times, frequently, the lack of available help makes it advisable for you to phone ahead to be sure that the place you select for a meal is open and at what hours."

Martha Work Ashelman remembered these war years as being rather difficult and described what it was like to grow up in Santa Cruz in the 1940s. Martha's mother was Geraldine G. Work, the city-county librarian from 1940 to 1968, who is known for coordinating the reconstruction of the Downtown branch of the library as well as the Branciforte branch of the library. Geraldine's salary was $160 a week. She was a widow who raised four children in one of the oldest houses in the city, which was located at 127 Green Street. Martha said, "There were a lot of fruit trees with several old pear trees, plus a Victory Garden on the property, with lots of tomato bushes." Martha continued, "My mother used to order her groceries by telephone from the old McHugh-Bianchi Market and pick them up on the way home. Her ration books may even have been kept there [for convenience]." Martha remembered that her mother enjoyed the abalone steaks at the Deer Park Tavern, which was on the way to Aptos, and she remembered that the family enjoyed eating at the Santa Cruz Hotel. Martha said, "[My siblings and I] went to Santa Cruz High

Pep Creameries matchbook. *Courtesy of Norman Davis.*

School, and every once in a while, would walk over to the Pep Creamery on Pacific Avenue for a milkshake in the afternoon."

In her autobiography, *Almost a Hundred Years*, Hulda Hoover McLean remembers the war years in the chapter "Some Side Effects of War, 1943–1946":

> *During the war, there were strict controls over what farmers could raise. Beans were a crop assigned to our area* [Rancho del Oso, sixteen miles north of Santa Cruz near Waddell Beach]. *Beans, however, usually mold in the coastal mist. Another permitted crop was cabbage. The armed forces used a lot of dehydrated cabbage. We decided to sharecrop cabbage…*[we] *planted seed, weeded, pulled and transplanted, fertilized and irrigated. With wartime labor restrictions, we did most of the work ourselves, with the help of the boys, and occasional farmworkers. War rationing and shortages of gasoline, food, equipment, labor, all of which were inconveniences in our farming, were devastating to the agricultural economy of the country as a whole at a time when food was critically needed all over the world.*

Santa Cruz had the tremendous advantage of being a fishing community with plenty of fresh seafood available in the Monterey Bay. In Michael Hemp's book *Cannery Row: The History of Old Ocean View Avenue*, he describes that the typical catch of local sardines measured, on average, eleven inches long (as opposed to the more preferable finger-length sardines found in the Atlantic Ocean). However, during the war years, and due to ration demands, the larger sardines were processed, canned and eaten anyway.

Al McLean, Hulda's youngest son, grew up at the Hoover Ranch—the Rancho del Oso. He went to Mission Hill Junior High School and Santa

Cruz High School. He remembers the Deer Park Tavern very well. "It was a steakhouse with a banquet room that was often used for the local high school proms—lots of wood paneling, a little too dark and a little dingy. But the bar was always loud and convivial—full of lawyers from around the area." John Hibble from the Aptos History Museum said:

> The Deer Park Tavern was built by N.J. (Shorty) Butriza, a Yugoslavian. The Tyrolean style building was originally decorated with hunting trophies, and the music was supplied by a Hammond organ built for the place. The widening of Highway One in the late 1940s forced Shorty to move it up the hill to its current location. The Tavern was jacked up about ten feet on stilts and moved horizontally up the hill, over and over, until it reached the top of the hill.

The Deer Park Tavern's newspaper ad said, "The old reliable, where your friends have met for years. You know us!"

Costella's Chalet was a very popular place in Felton, on Highway 9 in the San Lorenzo Valley. From 1941 to 1984, Costella's was described as "The Mecca" for dining and dancing on Saturday nights. Owner Lou Costella booked live Swing-Era bands to perform, and it became a showplace for great music; his sons, Bob and Edward, continued the tradition.

Dee Weybright recalled:

> In wartime, margarine was used instead of butter, and it came with a small packet of yellow dye, which as a kid, I enjoyed squeezing by hand into the stuff. There was kind of a barter system for us during those days—eggs and chickens were traded for sugar and so forth. If someone had a special birthday, for example, all the neighbors would pitch in to help with the ingredients for the cake and icing. In Soquel, we were used to raising rabbits and chickens, and there were plenty of fruit trees and blackberry bushes. We weren't as bad off as the folks in the big cities across America.

Len Klempnauer remembers rationing very well. "As kids, we had to carry our family's cans of kitchen grease and fat to school—it was collected there, and we all had to do it."

At its grand opening in 1928, the Casa del Rey Hotel was advertised as a "Show Spot." It was a famous destination for live music, with beautiful gardens, lovely patios and a large ballroom and dining room. During World War II, the United States Naval Administration considered the

DEER PARK TAVERN

Specializing in . . .
Broiled Steaks - Chops - Fried Chicken
N. J. BUTRIZA, Proprietor

DINE AND DANCE
PHONE APTOS 25
10 Miles From Watsonville
8 Miles From Santa Cruz
Watsonville-Santa Cruz Highway
Rio Del Mar, California

Deer Park Tavern, Aptos. advertisement in the March/April 1947 issue of *Tri-County Horseman. Author's collection.*

Costella's Chalet postcard. *Author's collection.*

Casa del Rey to be "a perfect fit" for rehabilitating the wounded. So, on March 9, 1943, the hotel was commissioned as a naval convalescent hospital. Two weeks later, it was ready for its new purpose and able to accommodate five hundred patients. According to the California State Military Museum, "The hospital experienced its busiest year in 1944, when 8,099 patients were received. In all, more than 18,600 men received convalescent services before the hospital was decommissioned on April 1, 1946." Patients recuperated in the sunshine and fresh air, and they enjoyed physical therapy in the indoor saltwater plunge across the street (now the Neptune's Kingdom). An expression often used in advertising this popular plunge and high dive was "Swim for Vim!" During the three years that the Casa del Rey was not operating as a hotel, nightclub or restaurant, it was still a good business for local commerce. It generated immediate sales of ice, restaurant supplies and locally grown and harvested food. Another source of revenue for the city were the local motels and hotels, where hospital personnel and the visiting families of patients needed to stay.

After the navy servicemen and hospital personnel left, the Casa del Rey was repainted, its bathrooms were remodeled and the gardens were cleaned up. On June 29, 1946, the hotel was once again ready again for vacationers and state conventions. Its cocktail lounge, the Il Trocadero, was also back in business, and a famous French chef was hired to oversee its new kitchen—Chef Alfred J. Bohn, who had trained under George Rector in New York. In 1947, the Miss California Pageant festivities came back to celebrate in Santa Cruz, and for many years, the final crowning ceremony was held in the Casa del Rey's huge ballroom. As advertised in 1957, the hotel's rates ranged from seven dollars to twenty dollars per night during the winter and from ten dollars to twenty-five dollars per night during the summer. After a few financial ups and downs, the Casa del Rey was repurposed, redecorated and converted into a 250-room retirement home in 1960. It remained an upscale retirement home until the 1989 earthquake, when it was red-tagged, leaving 147 residents displaced (although, thankfully, none of them were injured). Shortly afterward, the hotel had to be completely torn down, and it is now the main parking lot for the Santa Cruz Beach Boardwalk.

The Il Trovatore Hotel and Restaurant was located just west of the Casa del Rey, on the corner of Beach Street and Pacific Avenue, opposite the Municipal Wharf. It featured a "Modern Cocktail Lounge with par excellence Mixologist" and was owned by Pete Tori. It advertised that it served the finest Italian food, with a large selection of wines, and could easily handle large parties and banquets.

Casa del Rey Hotel, which was used as a naval convalescent hospital from 1943 to 1946. *Author's collection.*

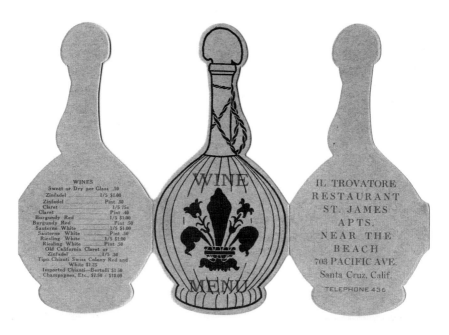

Il Trovatore Hotel wine list. Listed on the verso are more cocktails, including Slings, Fizzes and Flips. *Author's collection.*

In the early 1940s, located on the corner of Front and Laurel Streets, was the Father Divine Peace Restaurant. It was one of the few African American–owned restaurants in Santa Cruz County and was very much sought after by church community groups visiting from Oakland and San Francisco. An article in the *Santa Cruz Sentinel* dated July 5, 1940, reported that two hundred of Father Divine's church followers visiting from Oakland had a Fourth of July picnic in DeLaveaga Park. The Father Divine movement owned many restaurants nationwide. Vince Dixon discussed Father Divine's "tableside evangelism" in his well-written article "Heaven was a Place in Harlem." The property on 401 Front Street was renamed and remodeled a number of times after the Father Divine Peace Restaurant was closed. In October 1944, the restaurant Chicken Villa opened at the location, which was transformed into a drive-in. The Chicken Villa advertised that its fried chicken was ready to take out in boxes—perfect for beachgoers.

The original location of the Tea Cup was 11 Pearl Alley, but that location was closed in 1943, when Dan Y. Yee joined the army. After coming home from the war, Dan and his wife, Rose, reopened their business and moved the Tea Cup to the second floor of The Plaza Bakery in May 1946. The May 12, 1946 issue of the *Santa Cruz Sentinel* reported, "The main dining room overlooks the five streets which converge there and has a capacity for fifty to sixty persons. An unusual feature is the Shangri-La Room, available for small parties, such as club committee meetings." Al McLean recalls, "The bar was very popular with the downtown business crowd. It was

Chicken Villa ad in the *Santa Cruz Sentinel* on May 31, 1947. *Author's collection.*

definitely my dad's favorite bar. The cuisine was very good—not greasy and was well-presented, featuring standard Chinese-American dishes. The owner always gave the girls a fresh rosebud." The Tea Cup was sold in January 1957 to Don J. Yee (no relation) and his partners Wilbert Lum and Leon Lee. Christina Waters said, "The Tea Cup was legendary—known as the 'in' place downtown, with deep velour chairs and couches and a lively bar." Leo Stefani said, "I used to walk up the red staircase and always see Skip Littlefield sitting at the end of the bar." Skip Littlefield was the publicist for the Santa Cruz Beach Boardwalk, the emcee for the Miss California Pageant, the director of the Santa Cruz Chamber of Commerce and a regular columnist for the *Santa Cruz Sentinel*.

The entire Flatiron Building, including the Tea Cup and The Plaza Bakery, was red-tagged and slated for demolition after the 1989 Loma Prieta earthquake. Steve Hosmer recalls going past the surrounding chain link fence

Tea Cup matchbook.
Author's collection.

and up the staircase of the Tea Cup restaurant shortly after the earthquake. "I saw tables still set up with dinner plates full of food, untouched—it was as if the customers had just been served, but they got up and walked away—ran away, actually." Steve rescued the restaurant's two main signs: "Tea Cup" (mounted on an outside wall of his family's home) and "Restaurant" (on display at his business, Stokes Signs, in Santa Cruz). "They're really heavy. My professional guess is they were originally made in the 1940s, commissioned by Dan Y. Yee and were done by the Santa Cruz Electrical Company, located on Soquel Avenue in Santa Cruz....The lettering style and overall design is so similar to their other work."

A popular ice cream and soda fountain shop was the College Daze Cafe on Pacific Avenue, owned and operated by a Greek-American man named Harry Papalian from 1937 to 1946. The *Santa Cruz Sentinel*'s description when it opened said, "Decorations of the place are in blue and white, with an undergraduate motif in mind." The menu was printed on one side only.

The Saddle Rock Cafe and Coffee Shop was located inside the St. George Hotel on Pacific

Above: Saddle Rock Cafe advertisement. *Courtesy of Norman Davis.*

Left: College Daze Tavern menu from the early 1940s. *Author's collection.*

Opposite: Ship Ahoy postcard. "Overlooking the beautiful Monterey Bay and famous Santa Cruz Casino and bathing beach. Glass enclosed dining room and marine view banquet hall." *Author's collection.*

Avenue. George J. Carstulovich was its manager, and several social clubs and charitable organizations held their regular meetings there. Inside the hotel was the beautiful Palm Court, with its mosaic floors and a large Spanish-style fountain. The dining room was decorated in a colonial Spanish style and could seat up to two hundred guests.

The Ship Ahoy (also called the Ship) was located at the east entrance of the Santa Cruz Municipal Wharf, and it featured a life-size replica of a ship's prow—it was the perfect opportunity for a snapshot. The Ship was first owned by George H. Goebel and Anton Suk before it was sold to J.L. Olivieri and Angelo Rossi. Leo Stefani remembered, "There was a backdoor off from the kitchen and, for a quarter, Angelo would sell you a bag of fried clams." The patrons enjoyed views of the Monterey Bay and ordered bowls of homemade clam chowder—red or white.

The "Ship Ahoy"

GOEBEL & SUK
OWNER MANAGEMENT

DELICIOUS
SEA FOOD DINNERS
AND SALADS

ON THE BEACH
SANTA CRUZ, CALIF.

The Trout Farm Inn in Felton is an ideal fishing spot as well as a perfect location for a restaurant, and it's just seven miles from downtown Santa Cruz. Since 1906, the Trout Farm Inn was advertised as one of the first commercial trout farms in California. In 1944, Bill Fischer came back from serving in World War II, worked at the Brookdale Lodge for a brief time and, in 1946, purchased the five-acre Trout Farm Inn situated on the Zayante Creek. The Trout Farm Inn's main tourist attraction was the fresh spring-fed pond that the owner stocked each year with thousands of rainbow trout. It provided so much fun for families (no fishing license was required, and all of the tackle and fishing rods were furnished); and customers paid by the inch for the fish they caught. During the summer, guests stayed in motel units, ate fresh trout at the inn's restaurant and listened to music in the cocktail lounge. Even in the 1940s, the Trout Farm Inn sponsored a softball team. In general, sponsoring youth and adult sports teams (softball, football and soccer) was terrific advertising for restaurants; getting the name of a restaurant in the local newspaper for the length of the season—week after week—was a really good investment. In the late 1950s, Fischer added a heated outdoor swimming pool to the place. The Trout Farm Inn restaurant and resort had numerous owners and managers over the years, but it unfortunately suffered through a couple of bad fires and eventually closed.

Another longtime wharf restaurant was the Miramar Fish Grotto. It was in business from 1941 to 2015, and in April 2019, the building was finally razed to the ground. Jermaine Hunter was a sophomore at Santa Cruz High School in the early 1990s when he was hired at the Miramar. Jermaine is now a website developer (many of his customers are restaurants in Santa Cruz) and currently lives in San Diego. Jermaine said:

> *Charles Marcenaro hired a few of us basketball players, including my older brother Jesse (also known as "Champ"). I think he commiserated with us athletes. We were just sixteen and eighteen years old, and it was a good introduction into the working world. Charles had pretty much grown up there since he was a baby—his parents had run the Miramar for so many years.*

Charles Marcenaro Jr. played varsity basketball and varsity baseball at Santa Clara University, and for a time, he was an outfielder with the minor-league team of the Chicago Cubs. Jermaine said, "We called Charles's wife, Barbara, 'the Boss.' She always came down to meet Charles for dinner at closing time. I remember it just being so busy there. Live jazz music on the deck, Thursday night was lobster night and, of course, working the Christmas parties."

During their lunch and dinner shifts, while they were either waiting tables or tending bar, Jesse "Champ" Hunter and Steve Pollock, the author's husband, enjoyed putting their fishing rods out on the side railing; they kept close watch for any action on their lines. Jermaine recalled:

> *Once, when it was storming out and the waves were huge, a longtime bartender grabbed a surfboard off the wall that was used for displaying margarita prices or something and hopped out of the big window in the bar and over the back side of the wharf. He caught a wave all the way into Cowell's Beach. We were all stunned. He ran back to the Miramar on the wharf all dripping wet—and finished his shift!*

POPULAR DRINKS OF THE 1940s

Gin Rickey: In a Highball glass full of ice, pour two ounces of Gin, three-quarters of an ounce of lime juice, fill up with seltzer water; garnish with a lime wheel.

This cocktail was invented in the late nineteenth century in Washington, D.C., by Joe Rickey, a politician from Missouri. His recipe used Rye Whiskey, but over the years, bartenders replaced it with Gin. This drink is thirst quenching, with no sugar used at all in the recipe, unlike the Collins cocktails.

Mai Tai: In a cocktail shaker, pour two ounces of dark Rum, one-third of an ounce of simple syrup, one-half of an ounce of orange Curaçao, one-half of a lime, one-fourth of an ounce of Orgeat (almond) syrup. Shake and pour into an Old-fashioned glass filled with ice; garnish with the spent lime rind, a wedge of fresh pineapple and a cherry.

Victor Bergeron invented the Mai Tai in San Francisco in 1944. He was in the right place at the right time; he capitalized on the returning servicemen who remembered the South Sea island ambiance, music and décor. The Tiki craze in restaurant design was universal, and the Sāba in Capitola was a perfect example. In 1953, Victor Bergeron was hired by the Matson Steamship Line to help design the bar at its newest hotel, the Royal Hawaiian in Waikiki. He made over his original Mai Tai recipe by adding local, fresh pineapple juice and an extra floater of dark Rum. His book Trader Vic's

Matchbooks from Roudell's Restaurant and Coffee Shop, Hotel Palomar Coffee Shop and Cocktail Lounge and the Casa del Rey Hotel. *Cocktails prepared by author. Photograph by author. Author's collection.*

Helluva Man's Cookbook claims that the Mai Tai is his original recipe and calls the poachers a "bunch of lousy bastards for copying my drink." Victor Bergeron's favorite and signature technique is to use shaved ice. The Mai Tai celebrated its seventy-fifth birthday in 2019.

Sidecar: In a cocktail shaker filled with ice, pour two ounces of Cognac, one ounce of orange liqueur (Cointreau), one-half of an ounce of lemon juice, one-half of an ounce of simple syrup and a splash of fresh lime juice. Shake and strain into a Stem glass frosted with a light dusting of powdered sugar on the rim (optional); garnish with an orange slice.

This is a fun cocktail to watch being made and tastes delicious. It originated in Paris in the 1920s and was named after the motorcycle sidecar.

Chapter 2

The 1950s

CAR HOPS AND DRIVE-INS

In the 1950s, Santa Cruz County continued to be one of the most popular tourist destinations on the West Coast. At the time, the Census recorded that the population of Santa Cruz County was 66,534, including the many servicemen and women who came home from World War II and reentered their communities. Brochures described Santa Cruz as a place "where one can see the giant redwoods and the seashore in a matchless scenic setting." After the frugal war years, the people of Santa Cruz County were weary from having to watch every nickel they spent on gas, and now was the opportunity to enjoy "car culture" to the fullest (which certainly helped the local car dealerships). People liked car hops and drive-ins, first as a novelty, and then they got used to not having to get out of their cars for a meal, but they are especially remembered for their lively atmospheres. Many people wanted to show off their newly waxed cars and enjoy creamy chocolate milkshakes while listening to their favorite songs on the radio.

When carhop trays were first produced, they were made of pressed aluminum. The tray was invented by William L. McGinley, the president of Tray Service Co., and they were made by the Traco Manufacturing Company in Dallas, Texas. The Dallas Historical Society has a copy of the patent for the carhop tray invented and recorded by McGinley. Penny Castillo, the archivist librarian, said, "Coincidentally, my office is located just a couple of blocks away from the old address of the Traco Manufacturing Company!" McGinley's tray was a popular choice because it was lightweight and of a manageable size. It had a clip that also held the paper receipt. At

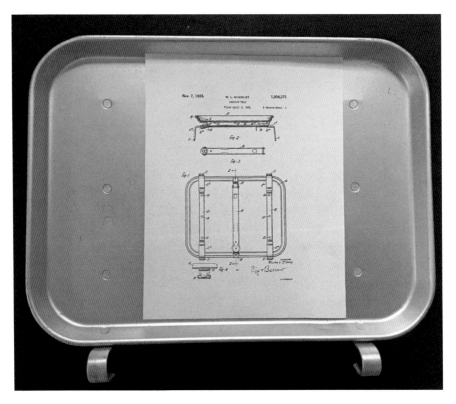

Photograph of an original carhop tray with a copy of its patent laid on it. *Patent office #1934271A. Photograph by author. Author's collection.*

first, there was a paper placemat to set on the top of the tray; later restaurants ordered thin, washable corrugated rubber mats that were designed for better traction. The tray had special brackets underneath that the carhop would place on a car door's window. Also available were short rubber sleeves (to prevent the glass from being scratched) in a variety of colors. McGinley also invented an *Automatic Bun Grill*, a *Motor-driven Bun Roller* and a *Bun Toaster.* McGinley, William L., inventor; Service Tray. Nov. 7, 1933. Filed and issued April 2, 1951. US patent 1,934,271.

For restaurant owners, offering a carhop service was a terrific way to increase their number of "tables," because if the inside area was full of customers, then the parking lot provided a perfect extension of service space and was a great way to increase business. Each carhop waitress would take an order, bring it back out and collect money from the customers—and maybe receive tips that she didn't have to report.

Len Klempnauer's parents, Leonard and Louise, came to Santa Cruz in 1946 and opened The Cross Roads Drive-In. The round landmark building was at the intersection of four streets: Washington Street, Pacific Avenue, West Cliff Drive and Center Street. Len said:

My dad, Leonard, built a huge brick barbecue outside and made his own barbecue sauce marinade. The tourist train dropped off passengers in front of the Boardwalk, but they departed back home from the Southern Pacific Depot right next door. Then, the line out front was really long—they could smell the delicious barbecue before getting back on board the train to go home! We were open until midnight during the winter and 3:00 a.m. during the summer. I started to wash dishes when I was twelve years old, mopped floors and peeled potatoes—it was such hard work! We had carhop service, and the girls wore their own slacks, blouses and [sweaters if it was foggy at night.] Our busiest nights were the Fourth of July and Labor Day weekends. Everything was cooked to-order; if it was hot weather, the milkshake machines were going non-stop.

Louise Klempnauer working the milkshake machine at The Cross Roads Drive-In. *Photograph courtesy of Len Klempnauer.*

The jukebox was inside, so radio speakers were hung up outside under the eaves to play the Top 40 songs, another inexpensive cost outlay with a maximum return. Len recalls:

The jukebox was rented, and the company's guy came once a month to switch out and put in the latest 45 records. It was really the greatest social scene; guys were "Cruisin' the Drag" (also known as Pacific Avenue, which, back then, went in both directions). People would eat at our place and then would drive on over to Spivey's 5-Spot on Ocean Street, or vice versa.

Len continued, "I played basketball and softball in high school and luckily didn't have to work on game nights. We played teams from the San Lorenzo Valley, Watsonville, Monterey and Salinas High Schools." The team mascots were (and still are) the Santa Cruz Cardinals, the San Lorenzo Cougars, the Watsonville Wildcatz, the Monterey Toreadors and the Salinas Vikings. Len said, "Sometimes, we stopped in at the Pronto Pup Drive-In [in Watsonville] on the way home. My dad sold our place in 1960, and then it became Danny's Drive-In, then it was Lighthouse Liquors for a long time." The building is now an office space.

Nita Gizdich of the Gizdich Ranch in Watsonville was a waitress at the Donut Den in Watsonville.

I started there in 1952, was recently married, and we lived across the street. I arrived at 7:00 a.m. every morning and worked until 12:00 p.m., went home to have lunch, do chores, et cetera, and then went back to the Donut Den from 3:00 p.m. to 5:00 p.m. I didn't have a uniform, but I wore a little apron. I was the dishwasher, waitress and helped at the counter, too. It was always busy around 10:00 a.m., when a crowd of utility workers came in then. In the afternoon, it was filled with kids from the high school a block away. I worked there for one year. The owners were such nice people.

Sam Leask is the director of philanthropic services for the Community Foundation of Santa Cruz County. He is a fifth-generation native of Santa Cruz and graduated from Santa Cruz High School. Sam remembers going out with his friends to Spivey's 5 Spot on Ocean Street for their Broasted Chicken. "Spivey's was so great—delicious food. It had a high-pitched roof line, Googie-style, and their jukebox played all the latest music." The family business, Leask's Dept. Store on Pacific Avenue, was located in the heart of downtown across from the Cooper House. Sam said, "My father

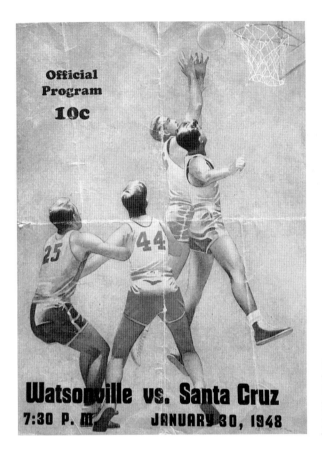

Official
Program
10c

Watsonville vs. Santa Cruz

7:30 P. M.   JANUARY 30, 1948

Santa Cruz High School versus Watsonville High School basketball game program, January 30, 1948. *Courtesy of Norman Davis.*

would often take his clients out for lunch at the Santa Cruz Hotel or to the Riverside Hotel."

Al McLean recalls:

> *On weekends, my buddies and I would cruise the drag endlessly trying to pick up girls. If we were lucky, we would take them to the 5 Spot for cokes and burgers. There was never a time when it was not busy. The folks at Pep Creamery were big boosters with the Santa Cruz High School (SCHS); photos of sports moments were plastered all over the walls. They also sold the local newspapers and sold comic books, too—it was usually packed. The color scheme was done in SCHS Cardinal red and white. I especially liked the strawberry shakes served with real whipped cream.*

The Riverside Hotel was located on the corner of Barson and Riverside. The hotel and its gardens originally covered about thirty acres of land and

Left: Riverside Hotel matchbook. *Courtesy of Norman Davis.*

Right: Zanze's Rocky Falls menu. *Courtesy of Jay Topping.*

faced the San Lorenzo River, but it was subdivided and remodeled a few times during the 1940s. The hotel's bar was called the Hunter's Cocktail Lounge. Al McLean said, "They had a huge dining room area and catered to the summer crowd. It was a pretty good summer job for high school students, although everyone joked that their 'chicken' was really seagull."

Al McLean also remembered, "Zanze's Rocky Falls Restaurant, on the way to Scotts Valley, had an excellent dining room that was big enough for hosting large parties, such as high school functions. Sam Zanze was a classmate of mine at Santa Cruz High School and a fellow member of the Honor Society." Zanze's was a popular place for booking all kinds of award dinners and holiday banquets. Zanze's was one of the places where the Elks, Masons and Rotary groups met every month. It was also famous for its homemade cheesecake. Leo Stefani said, "Louie Zanze was a terrific cook."

Young children are so impressionable; being taken out to eat at a "formal" restaurant is rather exciting for them, and often, these memories are long-lasting and indelible. Mary Murphy's maternal side of her family is the Leibbrandts, one of the oldest established families in Santa Cruz. Mary went to Holy Cross. Frank Murphy Sr., Mary's father, had his law office right next door to the St. George Hotel. Mary remembered, "I remember our family often ate inside at the Saddle Rock Cafe. It was a little bit formal—a little dark—with very good food. The manager, George Carstulovich, was just like family and a real good friend of my dad." The film actress Zazu Pitts lived upstairs in the hotel for many years. Mary is a member of Research Anonymous of Santa Cruz County.

Linda and her husband, Steve Page, have lived in Santa Cruz for over fifty years. She remembers that they would often go to Spivey's 5 Spot after a movie. She said, "They had the best onion rings—light as a feather—fabulous!" Spivey's opened in 1951; in 1970, the site became Jay's Restaurant, and it is now a two-story bank building. In the 1960s, another Spivey's opened up in the then-new East Cliff Shopping Center on Seventeenth Avenue and East Cliff Drive; this location featured the same fresh baked goods and Broasted Chicken, and it was open for twenty-four hours a day.

Mary P. Carniglia is recognized as possibly the very first female restaurant owner in Santa Cruz County. In the early 1940s, she owned and operated the Miramar Fish Grotto on the wharf, Carniglia's on the wharf and then the Riviera Restaurant and Hotel on 144 Pacific Avenue. The Riviera was open for business on Friday, Saturday and Sunday, and it specialized in classic Italian cuisine, featuring Mary's recipes. She is also remembered for her kindness toward Italian immigrants during and after World War II. She dedicated many hours to volunteering as an interpreter and translator, helping many people with their paperwork and citizenship forms.

Virginia Poulos was a carhop waitress at Carroll's Drive-In (in Watsonville) from 1955 to 1959. She recalls, "My boss bought our matching uniforms at Joseph Magnin's—we were the best dressed carhops ever! Friday night was race night at the Watsonville Fairgrounds, and we were always so busy! Loved the job; it sold, but I continued working there until 1963."

Leo Stefani remembered a Spivey's 5 Spot story from the early 1950s:

I was there with Norman Gotti, who ran cattle up the coast, and Brad Macdonald of Sāba's, when late one night, Carl Ravazza [the famous tenor and orchestra leader also known as Carl Ravell] *came in. We moved all of the furniture back against the walls and made a dance*

Left: Spivey's 5 Spot telephone book advertisement from 1955. "Broasted" means that the chicken pieces are cooked in a high temperature pressure fryer; the technique seals in the juices and makes the outside crispy. *Author's collection.*

Right: Carroll's Drive-In advertisement. *Courtesy of Norman Davis.*

floor. Norman went out to his car and got his accordion—he played his accordion and Carl sang. It was really a memorable night, I'll never forget it! Then came the flood in 1955, with the high water coming in on one side and running out the other. Water was clear up over the parking meters! Just killed the place.

Leo Stefani told a story about the Colonial Inn.

In 1949, someone at the Santa Cruz Credit Bureau called Don (my brother) and said, "We heard you're looking for a place!" Stan Hoffman sold it to Don in 1950. My sisters set up the smorgasbord or Seafoodorama on Fridays, and the waiting list was forever. Malio J. Stagnaro supplied everything, including steamed cockles clams that came in large wooden boxes from Washington state; delivered six hundred pounds of them. And lots of times, we were still serving at midnight! Don had Christmas presents made for special customers; gloves specially made for the ladies and wives of friends, and one year, even a large mirror. The owner of KSCO radio came in to make announcements from inside the restaurant.

Right: Colonial Inn mirror. It is approximately twenty inches tall and twelve inches wide. *Courtesy of Leo Stefani.*

Below: Colonial Inn menu and three postcards, circa the late 1950s. "The Firelight Room serving 'superb cocktails' until 2:00 a.m., nightly." *Author's collection.*

Carolyn Swift said:

> *In Capitola, the popular Esplanade restaurant for generations was the Bandstand, which started, literally, as a bandstand. Eventually, it was totally enclosed, and in 1959, the bandstand portion was demolished. To this day, however, old-timers reminisce about the flavor of Babe's fries. Everybody loved them. Babe was "Babe" Yakobovich—the secret to his fries was lamb lard!*

The Sāba in Capitola was built on the site of the old, magnificent Capitola Hotel, which was destroyed by a fire in 1929. Brad Macdonald and his father, Jack, bought the property (it had been a roller-skating rink for a while) and designed their nightclub in the style of the wildly popular Trader Vic's, the San Francisco institution. It had a grand opening in 1954. The Sailfish Room was decorated in classic Tiki, featuring an outrigger canoe. They advertised that their Caribbean Banquet Room could seat from one hundred to one thousand people and featured a huge dance floor, with a large stage and elaborate sound system. The Macdonalds booked big-name

The Bandstand, Capitola. *Photograph courtesy of the Capitola Historical Museum.*

Menu from the Sāba Club and Caribbean Ballroom, Capitola. *Courtesy of the Capitola Historical Museum.*

jazz musicians, including Dizzy Gillespie, Count Basie, Ella Fitzgerald and Lionel Hampton. Unfortunately, the Sāba and two adjoining buildings mysteriously burned to the ground on October 14, 1957.

Carolyn Swift recalls, "In Watsonville, Pronto Pup's most popular seller was their corndog. The establishment was owned by Dick and Lurine Crocker, who then went on to start the A&W restaurant franchise out on [1726] Freedom Boulevard." At their new place, the Crockers continued to sell their corndogs, which were also known as Pronto Pups, and swampwater, which was just a combination of root beer and orange soda. The old Pronto Pup building on Main Street is still there and is now the Tamal restaurant, which serves delicious homemade tamales. You can still see the drive-up window, but it's painted over, and the restaurant still has a large parking lot.

Carolyn also shared her memories of the Philippine Gardens Cafe in Watsonville. "The restaurant was owned by Rosita Tabasa-Estrada and had a card club in the back." The Tabasa family had owned it since 1938.

Pronto Pup's advertisement in the Watsonville High School *Manzanita* yearbook from 1958. *Courtesy of the Pajaro Valley Historical Association.*

When I was a kid, I lived around the corner, and their house always smelled fabulous. It lasted for over fifty years, until the 1989 Loma Prieta earthquake forced its closure. The cafe served authentic dishes, such as Dinuguan—pig intestine marinated in vinegar, spices and blood. It was also a center of local Filipino culture and a meeting place long before senior centers were created. It was included in a county history course at Cabrillo College and became a stop for students on ethnic tours. The couple also owned rental housing, a second restaurant, a pool hall and a barbershop. Mrs. Estrada worked closely with several Watsonville mayors as a community liaison, and represented Filipinos in groups such as Project Scout and the Equal Opportunity Commission. She worked on many local events, including the Fourth of July parade, political rallies, and held an annual Christmas party at the restaurant for customers and friends.

In a newspaper interview with Heron Marquez Estrada, dated 1985, titled "Philippine Gardens Cafe: It's more than just a card room," Rosita Tabasa-Estrada said that she was given the cafe as a wedding present by her in-laws. It soon became popular with migrant Filipino field workers who sought to escape the boredom of the dreary camps they lived in as they followed the crops along the coast.

Sharon Nystrom Watson and her husband, Frank Watson, both graduated from Santa Cruz High School in the early 1950s. She worked at the Coast Creamery, where ice cream was made fresh daily, for three years in the 1960s. Sharon said:

COAST CREAMERY

PASTEURIZED
DAIRY PPRODUCTS

FRENCH CUSTARD ICE CREAM

Fountain Service

SANTA CRUZ

Phone 390   359 Pacific Ave.

Coast Creamery advertisement. *Courtesy of Norman Davis.*

My friends and I would go to the two drive-ins, Spivey's 5 Spot on Ocean Street or to the Cross Roads up on Washington Street, on Fridays after the football games and on "date nights" on Saturdays. We ordered our burgers and fries outside from the carhop waitress, even on prom nights in our nicest dresses! Or if it was a cold night, we'd go inside and eat— there was always music on the jukebox, and we'd all dance.

There are thousands of stories about the disastrous flood of December 22, 1955. Dee Weybright remembers, "It was Christmas time—just pouring rain—but I had to go out and shop for a pair of red shoes! We drove our old Ford down the hill, and of all things, we saw a man in a rowboat! The water was that high!" Dee's husband, Art, said:

The next day, I helped to clear out the big logs from under the bridge at Soquel Drive that was creating the dam. It was pretty frustrating, and some of us wanted to use dynamite to blast it—let all that water go.

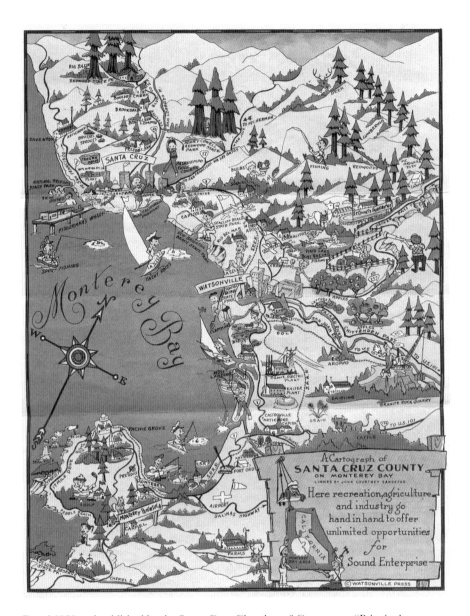

Dated 1959 and published by the Santa Cruz Chamber of Commerce. "Principal agricultural crops are lettuce, apples, cherries, artichokes, tomatoes, mushrooms, berries, bulbs and flowers." *Author's collection.*

Luckily, a guy in a big truck honked and honked and told us the city's main gas line went right through there! Stopped us just in time! It would have been a real disaster.

Previous days of heavy rains—between fourteen and eighteen inches a day—combined with a series of high tides meant that there was no outlet to the Monterey Bay. These conditions caused the water level of the San Lorenzo River to rise so high that it overflowed its banks and flooded the downtown area of Santa Cruz. There was no electricity and no telephone service for days; there were uprooted trees, debris and mud and silt everywhere on the streets. Shop owners along Pacific Avenue watched as the mud and the mess came through their doors and windows. The Avenue Grill, located on the corner of Pacific Avenue and Spruce Street, is an example of those that suffered interior damage all the way down to its basement, as did other stores and merchants in the downtown area. Whole neighborhoods and communities were changed forever, and nearly two thousand people were displaced. In the book *Santa Cruz County: A Century*, Donna Jones wrote, "The flooding was blamed in the deaths of eight people county-wide, and caused $7.5 million in damage to the city of Santa Cruz alone." A lot of changes were made to the city's infrastructure after the flood. The 1955 flood prompted the city to implement a U.S. Army Corps of Engineers flood control project to replace the riverbanks with rock and cement levees.

Jessie Durant, the archivist for the Seaside Company, said, "Ruth's Hamburger's was located at Entrance 3, across from the Carousel. The restaurant was opened by Ruth and Glen Hunter in 1938. In 1953, it was taken over by Victor Marini Jr., who kept the name and operated it for seventeen years. Today, the Seaside Company operates it as the Surf City Grill."

Gordon's Chuck House was on the corner of Scotts Valley Drive and Mt. Hermon Road and opened in 1955. They advertised that they had a television, and invited customers to come "watch boxing nightly in the Lariat Lounge." Dinners at Gordon's Chuck House were served "Chuck Wagon Style," and many Scotts Valley Chamber of Commerce meetings were held there. In the late 1960s, during the baseball season, the restaurant ran a round-trip bus to the San Francisco Giants games for ten dollars, and that included a meal.

The Brookdale Lodge is located up on Highway 9, approximately twelve miles from downtown Santa Cruz. It has a wild history; it has

Avenue Grille after the December 1955 flood. *Courtesy of Norman Davis.*

Ruth's Hamburgers and the Santa Cruz Beach Boardwalk in the 1950s. *Author's collection.*

The lounge inside the Santa Cruz Elks Lodge #824 features a large black-and-white aerial photograph of Santa Cruz, which was taken by Pete Amos in 1958. Amos donated the photograph to the lodge. It is approximately ten feet tall and twelve feet wide. *Photograph by author. Courtesy of the Santa Cruz Elks Lodge #824.*

been through many financial highs and lows, various owners and strange stories of supposed hauntings. There are several books written on the purported paranormal activity surrounding the lodge. The story goes that a ten-year-old girl named Sarah Logan, the niece of the lodge's owner, Judge James Harvey Logan, slipped and fell on the rocks in the creek and died. Investigative reporters have interviewed guests and employees who claimed they saw a little girl appear and run through the hallways. The lodge was also a famous getaway vacation spot for Hollywood celebrities, such as Joan Crawford, Marilyn Monroe, Tyrone Power and President Herbert Hoover, who enjoyed fishing off the dining room bridge. President Hoover's niece, Hulda Hoover McLean, and her family lived nearby at the Rancho del Oso, and he may have been visiting them. The Brookroom features a natural stream running through the center of its dining room, and it was advertised that one could be married right there near the stream. Leo Stefani remembers going to

Above: Advertisement from Gordon's Chuck House, Scotts Valley. *Courtesy of Norman Davis.*

Left: A Brookdale Lodge matchbook. Built in 1922, the lodge was famous as a getaway spot for Hollywood celebrities, and it is said to be haunted by ghosts. *Courtesy of Norman Davis.*

the lodge after a big storm: "I went to meet up with some friends and saw mud piled up two feet high in the bar! The kitchen had the biggest, fanciest dishwasher I've ever seen in a private establishment." The lodge is currently being renovated by its new owner.

In the late 1950s, there was a countywide vote to build a junior college, now known as Cabrillo Community College. (One suggestion was that it be named Begonia College, which would have been a lovely reflection of the neighboring city's popular Capitola Begonia Festival.) Classes began in 1959, with an enrollment of 400 students at the Aptos campus. The school's 1990 course catalog listed that 13,027 students were enrolled. In 1976, Cabrillo began to offer a Food Services Technology Program, under the direction of Tom King (owner of the Courtyard Restaurant). The program is now called the Culinary Arts and Hospitality Program.

Top: Brookdale Lodge advertisement in a Miss California Pageant program from 1958. *Author's collection.*

Bottom: 1957 Santa Cruz Chamber of Commerce brochure. "Spectacular scenery—from scenic West Cliff Drive to Big Basin State Park." *Author's collection.*

POPULAR DRINKS OF THE 1950s

Cuba Libre: In a Highball glass full of ice, pour two ounces of light Rum, squeeze half of a fresh lime (leaving rind on top), fill with cola and garnish with the other half of lime.

In the 1950s, the Cuba Libre was a standard drink order and remains today as one of the top ten. The recipe began as an echo of the rallying cry for Cuban independence in 1900, and it continued to be a big hit during World War II, helped a great deal because of the famous tune sung by the Andrews Sisters.

Perfect Manhattan: In a cocktail shaker full of ice, pour two ounces of Bourbon, one-half ounce of dry Vermouth and one-half ounce of sweet Vermouth; two dashes bitters; shake and strain into a Coupe glass (chilled if desired); garnish with an orange slice and a cherry.

Vermouth is an ideal mixer, consisting of approximately 75 percent alcohol, with an added variety of aromatics and herbs, plus sugar. The equal parts of dry and sweet Vermouth used in the Perfect Manhattan make for a balanced taste.

Matchbooks from Gordon's Chuck House, Colonial Inn and Locatelli's Inn. *Cocktails prepared by author. Photograph by author. Author's collection.*

Tom Collins: In a Collins glass filled with ice, pour two ounces of dry Gin, two ounces of fresh lemon juice and one ounce of simple syrup; stir and fill with seltzer; garnish with a lemon wedge.

A refreshing drink invented by Jerry Thomas in the nineteenth century, the Tom Collins contains the three basics: the sour (lemon), the sweet and the liquor, topped with seltzer water. A John Collins uses Bourbon instead of Gin.

Chapter 3

The 1960s

CREDIT CARDS AND UCSC

In the 1960s, the Census recorded that the population of Santa Cruz County was 84,219—nearly double the size of its population recorded in the 1940s. People born between 1946 and 1964 are often described as the "Baby Boom Generation," and in retrospect, members of this generation helped to shape long-lasting trends.

More American consumers were paying for travel expenses with credit cards, perhaps treating the family at dinner to the fresh-caught salmon or a bottle of local California wine, exclaiming, "After all, we are on vacation!" Accepting credit cards made dining out easier for the non-cash-carrying customer to act on impulse and splurge on themselves—or if it was a business lunch meeting, on their clients. Because Santa Cruz was (and is) a tourist destination, many restaurants promoted this convenient way to pay and printed the slogan and illustration right on the menu. The colorful and eye-catching decals that said, "We Accept Credit Cards" (provided by the banks) were placed on front doors and windows of establishments. When a customer finished their meal, a waitperson or hostess would take a credit slip paper draft form and slide the customer's credit card back and forth over a non-electronic, manual credit card imprint machine before returning to the table for the customer to sign the copies, handing him one to keep. (This transaction is always a little tricky, the rule being, whoever handed you the card, hand it back to that person.) These were the early years of non-cash transactions, when both owners and employees had to adjust to the impacts that credit cards had on their businesses.

Diners' Club Inc. began promoting its credit card in the early 1950s, and it was quickly followed by American Express. Merchants and restaurants realized that the use of these cards was a tremendous convenience for the tourist crowd. It was just one more detail that the wait staff had to pay attention to; checking to see that the correct amount had been filled out (hopefully with a gratuity) was very important. Credit card slips had to be signed legibly, and in later years, customers were required to leave a phone number. The next day's bank deposit would have to include every credit slip, along with the checks and cash. After a few days, restaurants would be paid the amount they deposited minus a percentage for the new opportunity of accepting credit cards. Customers who used their credit cards would receive a bill in the mail the following month. Ted Burke of the Shadowbrook in Capitola recalled when credit cards were first used. "Each week, the card companies [Diners' Club, AmEx, Visa and Mastercard] sent out booklets with all of the numbers and names of fraudulent cards. Our hostesses and servers checked thoroughly, but if we didn't catch it in time, we were stuck with not being paid."

Dino Stagnaro of Gilda's on the Santa Cruz Municipal Wharf said, "We didn't take credit cards until the early 1980s, but we had to start because people were used to it and preferred it instead of cash. Then, we had to carefully check through the little magazines the banks gave out, searching for each name. Now, the computer has made that easier, and the payment goes through right away!"

Credit card imprint machine. *Photograph by author. Author's collection.*

A major impact to the Santa Cruz County area came in the fall of 1965, when students and faculty arrived at the new University of California (UC) campus, the University of California at Santa Cruz, which was built on the site of the old Cowell Ranch. The starting enrollment was only 637 undergraduate students. In June 1969, the school's enrollment was up to 3,713 students, which included graduate students. While on campus, students and the faculty ate in the dining halls or at the Whole Earth Restaurant or, if they were feeling adventurous, drove down the hill to eat downtown or discover new restaurants all over the county.

Rita Bottoms came to Santa Cruz in 1965, and she served as the head of Special Collections of the Library of the University of California, Santa Cruz until her retirement in 2003. While there, Rita established many culturally influential archives and curated many important collections. She said, "We took Arnold Fawcus of the *Trianon Press*, [who was] visiting Santa Cruz at the time, to L'Oustalou, and we all enjoyed the dinner there immensely." Rita said she often went to "the old Rexall Drugs lunch counter on Mission Street for their ordinary, but delicious, sandwiches."

Traci Bliss, born at the original Sister's Hospital, is the fifth generation of the Moses Bliss family to live in Santa Cruz. She is the co-author of *Santa Cruz's Seabright*. She recalled, "So many of us went to Manoff's Rancho Burger on Friday nights, then on to a movie at the Del Mar. If my mother went shopping at Leask's Dept. Store, she would first park us kids at the soda fountain inside Melvin's Drug Store on Pacific Avenue. What a treat!"

In 1964, the hit song "Under the Boardwalk" was recorded by The Drifters and was ranked number four on the charts. Written by Kenny Young and Arthur Resnick, the lyrics may have been inspired by Coney Island, but the song is universally loved and is certainly a favorite on the Boardwalk in Santa Cruz.

Melinda Facelli said she started working at her family's restaurant, helping to check coats and hats, when she was ten years old. Her family lived on Lighthouse Avenue near La Barranca Park. Her dad, Louie Facelli, had been a one-third owner of the Santa Cruz Hotel, along with John Righetti and Don Stefani. She said, "Then, he saw an opportunity to take over Micossi's on the West Side of Santa Cruz. It was sandwiched in between Wrigley's Gum and the Lipton Tea factory."

One of the largest employers in the city of Santa Cruz was the Wrigley's Chewing Gum Manufactory on Mission Street, built in 1953. At the time, it was the largest Wrigley plant west of the Mississippi. People remember the changing aromas in the air—a fruity smell on some days, and on other days, it was mint. The gum factory closed its doors in 1997.

Melinda continued: "Dad added on the huge banquet room with a separate entrance and its own bar and restrooms." Facelli's was *the* place to go in Santa Cruz from 1959 to 1973. Leo Stefani was the chef for awhile, and Leo Grigorio was the maître d' at Facelli's. Melinda remembered:

> *At first, they didn't serve lunch, just dinner. There were plenty of big award parties, one even hosting Mrs. Governor Pat Brown, and lots of bachelor parties and wedding receptions. Dad enjoyed hosting charity events, serving his famous venison scallopini, since he was an avid hunter. He butchered it in the kitchen. He enjoyed holding talent shows to raise money for the local Santa Cruz Elks Lodge #824.*

Melinda remembers her dad often helped his employees. "There was a man who played the organ in the bar, and Dad gave him the money, outright, for a car." Melinda's father also had the gift of gab. "People came from miles around just for his personality. His family came from the Tramonti region of Italy, and my mom was 100 percent Portuguese. Mom was the hostess on weekends and brought all the accounting home. I still have her little desk and use it in my own office."

Bruce McPherson is a fifth-generation native of Santa Cruz; his family owned the local newspaper, the *Santa Cruz Sentinel*, for many years. Bruce is currently the Santa Cruz County Supervisor for the Fifth District. He said:

> *My mother's favorite restaurant was the old Santa Cruz Hotel for their classic Italian food. And Castagnola's was really top notch; it was a place where dining out was truly a social experience. My grandmother lived in Ben Lomond, and the family used to love going out to the old Locatelli's, now Scopazzi's.*

One of Santa Cruz's oldest restaurants was the Santa Cruz Hotel, which was highly regarded for its traditional Italian food and friendly atmosphere. It was once a boardinghouse known as the Germania Hotel and was in a good location because it was just a short walk from the railroad depot. The Santa Cruz Hotel has had several owners, beginning in 1928 with Stella Pera. Then, in the 1940s, business partners John Righetti, Louie Facelli and Don Stefani bought it; they were followed by George H. Goebel and Anton Suk. Al Castagnola, Friend (Amigo) Arevalo and Annie Righetti took over

Above: Postcard featuring Facelli's dining room. *Author's collection.*

Left: Facelli's sugar cube. *Photograph by author. Courtesy of Norman Davis.*

in the 1950s and 1960s, and they were followed by Frank Cardinale and then various other business partnerships. Patrons could order authentic Cioppino for takeout, as well as their raviolis, which were made upstairs by Annie Righetti.

Downstairs was the Crown Room, which was famous for its bright red, flocked wallpaper and for being decorated with portraits of the winners of the Miss California Pageant. In a special, locked glass case was the official crown and several other historic items from the pageant. Al Castagnola, Skip Littlefield and the Santa Cruz Beach Boardwalk were instrumental in promoting this event, which started in Santa Cruz in 1924. Then it was held in San Francisco and Venice, California, from 1925 to 1946. The pageant returned to Santa Cruz in 1947 and remained until 1985. During the 1980s, there were loud protests and marches in the streets against the pageant,

Santa Cruz Hotel cocktail napkin. *Courtesy of Norman Davis.*

which used the slogan "Myth California," so the pageant committee decided to relocate to San Diego before finally settling in Fresno.

Dr. Paul A. Lee remembers when he and his good friend Page Smith would often go for lunch at the Santa Cruz Hotel. "As soon as we'd come in, Annie Righetti walked right up to Page, wrapped her arms around him and lifted him way up off the floor—he loved it!" Leo Stefani said, "Annie was strong enough to lift one-hundred-pound sacks of flour for her raviolis. She made them upstairs on a huge table." In Annie's obituary, which is dated April 8, 2003, the *Santa Cruz Sentinel* stated, "Her brother John Righetti and Chef Rico Malatesta taught her the making of beef raviolis, which she turned out nine thousand raviolis daily, four days a week until she sold her share of the restaurant." Al McLean recalled, "When I was young, it was always a place to go for dining 'family-style,' beginning with a really great minestrone soup. The owner always kept the adults' wine glasses full."

In the 1970s, under new management, the upstairs was redecorated with big mirrors and beautiful, lush ferns and called the Santa Cruz Hotel Bar & Grille. One of its print ad campaigns was, "To Eat Upstairs Or Downstairs, That is The Question." The building suffered a great deal of damage during the 1989 earthquake (thankfully, it didn't have to come down) and went through months of interior and exterior repairs.

Marcia McDougal and her husband, Bruce, kept several photographs of the New Davenport Cash Store that were taken in the late 1960s. She said:

We started in 1967 with a total immersion, residential pottery school called Big Creek Pottery, where the students who enrolled in the nine-week workshops lived upstairs. The students' wares were sold downstairs, as well as my homemade muffins, freshly ground coffee and handmade coffee mugs, plates and other things. I made fresh soup every day in a gigantic crockery pot, which was plugged into the only outlet downstairs—in the bathroom! After a while, Bruce built us an actual kitchen, so we said, "Let's face it—we're a restaurant!" And Bruce hung up the sign. At that time, we

Santa Cruz Hotel Bar & Grille postcard. "The mood is casual, the hospitality is genuine and the cuisine is superb." *Author's collection.*

New Davenport Cash Store. *Courtesy of Marcia McDougal.*

served just lunch. Every morning, I'd go to Shopper's Corner for their meat and fresh fish.

We grew all of our own vegetables and raised our own chickens and pigs. A lot of bicyclists always stopped in—whole hungry teams! Davenport is only nine miles away from downtown Santa Cruz. Locals like Page and Eloise Smith [from Bonny Doon] *and the cement company employees were regulars, of course. We delivered to the cement plant, too. We washed and recycled everything that could be recycled! And we brought the leftover vegetable scraps home for the animals. The credit card machine was kept in the store, and we used it if folks didn't have cash. When Santa Cruz had the historic flood in 1982, we just turned on our generator—we were the only place that had one! In 1984, we bought the Whale City Bakery, and we still own that.*

After serving thirty to forty lunches a day, in addition to working in the pottery studio, Marcia and Bruce wanted to go into town to eat dinner. Marcia said, "Zanzibar's was very exotic—or we'd go to the Santa Cruz Hotel to see the bartender John Righetti. For something really adventurous, we'd go to the Pearl Alley Bistro; it had such a special aura—reminiscent of a European inn! We closed the New Davenport Cash Store in 1987."

NEW DAVENPORT CASH STORE
- BREAKFAST MENU -

OMELETS
3 EGGS, POTATOES,
FRESH PEDA BREAD

CHEESE	3.25
MUSHROOM	3.25
GREEN ONION	2.95
BEAN	2.95
COMBINATION VEGETABLE	3.25

HUEVOS RANCHEROS   2.95
TORTILLA, BEANS,
2 FRIED EGGS, MELTED CHEESE

HUEVOS TORTILLAS   2.95
3 EGGS SCRAMBLED WITH
DICED TORTILLAS, GREEN ONIONS,
MUSHROOMS & CHEDDAR CHEESE
— WITH BREAD: 3.25

TWO EGGS (ANY STYLE)   2.50
HOMESTYLE POTATOES
BREAD & BUTTER.

EGGS & WOK-STIRRED   2.95
VEGETABLES
PEDA BREAD & BUTTER.

SCRAMBLED TOFU   2.95
& VEGETABLES
PEDA BREAD & BUTTER.

TASTY ADDITIONS TO ANY ABOVE .50
CHOICE OF CHEESE,
TOMATO, GREEN ONION,
MUSHROOMS, SPROUTS, BEANS.

LUMBERJACK SPECIAL 3.95
- FRESH ORANGE JUICE
- 3 EGGS ANY STYLE
- 3 STRIPS BACON
- 3 PANCAKES
- COFFEE OR TEA   6:30-8:00

OUR OWN GRANOLA WITH MILK   1.35

BEVERAGES

FRESH GROUND COFFEE & REFILL	.50
BLACK TEA	.30
HERBAL TEA	.35
MILK	.60
ORANGE JUICE (FRESHLY SQUEEZED)	.95
APPLE JUICE	.55
TOMATO JUICE	.55
MINERAL WATER	.50

SIDE ORDERS

SAUSAGE, BACON	1.45
POTATOES	.90
YOGURT	.75
FRESH FRUIT COMPOTE	1.35

HOME BAKED GOODIES

CINNAMON ROLL	.90
MUFFIN	.60
BAGEL w/ BUTTER OR CREAM CHEESE	.75
HOME BAKED BREAD (2), BUTTER	.65
CHOCOLATE CHIP COOKIE BAR	.75
CARROT CAKE	.95
BROWNIE	.75

GOOD FOOD TAKES TIME TO COOK.
— EACH DISH IS INDIVIDUALLY
PREPARED TO YOUR ORDER.

FOOD TO TAKE OUT

426.4122

Above: Breakfast menu from New Davenport Cash Store. Teams of bicyclists considered this a breakfast destination on the weekends. *Courtesy of Marcia McDougal.*

Opposite, inset: Matchbook from The Sticky Wicket, Aptos. *Photograph by author. Courtesy of Norman Davis.*

Another rendezvous spot during the 1960s was The Sticky Wicket. Al McLean remembers the first Sticky Wicket location.

The Sticky Wicket first opened in 1959 as a coffeehouse in the back of Anderson's Music Store on Cathcart Street, near the Santa Cruz Bowl, which is now the Catalyst. For a year or so, it was the best jazz venue south of San Francisco; Freddie Gambrel on piano and Ben Tucker on bass was a steady gig there. Many names would drop in, like George Shearing and Art Blakely—the place was always jammed. Then the owners, Vic and Sidney Jowers, moved the place out to Aptos on Mar Vista Drive.

The menu featured really superbly cooked steaks, which were moderately priced, and they served great wines and imported beers. It was a hangout for intellectuals; actors; new-age musicians, like the great Lou Harrison and the early planners of the Cabrillo Festival of Contemporary Music; and local artists. It closed in 1964, when Cabrillo College built out that section of the freeway and because the owner Vic unfortunately passed away.

Al McLean remembers the Catalyst well. He said, "The Catalyst first opened in 1967 inside the St. George Hotel on 821 Front Street, with a delicatessen that served healthy, organic sandwiches with sprouts inside."

Sierra Prara is a second-generation Santa Cruz native who went to Harbor High School. She recalls going to the old Catalyst with her friends. "We went in there by first walking into Aries Arts and then through the sliding mirror doors." The Aries Arts store was famous for its "groovy" merchandise, such as Grateful Dead posters, bell-bottom pants, native-print bedspreads and wind chimes. Sierra said, "We'd sit near the fountain—with the goldfish swimming inside—surrounded by lots of plants, order tea and just hang out. Since we were just teenagers and underage, we weren't allowed inside the bar area, but we could still hear the bands. Moby Grape often played music there."

In 1976, Randall Kane, the Catalyst's owner, purchased the old bowling alley on Pacific Avenue and moved the Catalyst over there. He created a large and unique garden atrium, a fully equipped bar and a hugely popular nightclub. The Catalyst expanded upon its deli menu and began serving breakfast; it was especially busy on Sunday mornings. Visitors were always amazed by the huge, lifelike plaster elephant head that hung over the bar area; it had glowing red eyes and long tusks. The Catalyst also had a glass greenhouse roof and a lot of lush tropical plants in the dining room. On the south wall, there was a large, three-dimensional tile reproduction of Édouard Manet's 1882 painting *A Bar at the Folies-Bergère*. The Catalyst continues to be famous for being a premier music venue for rock and roll, folk, reggae and heavy metal bands on the West Coast.

Tom and Kathleen Manoff owned Manoff's Rancho Burger on the corner of Water and River Streets in downtown Santa Cruz. Tom said:

> *We were there for forty-two years—from 1959 to 2001. We had the only charcoal broiler in the city. A lot of our regular customers worked downtown, like the post office employees....We ordered our beef from Ledyard's. We had the broiler's grease cleaned regularly, every three months. We survived both the flood of 1982 and the 1989 earthquake. We lost a few plates, but Kathleen and I opened up the next day—no gas, but the broiler was okay. We even ran out of food!*

Geri Derpich Heebner's parents, Nick and Katie Derpich, were co-owners of the Miramar Bar and Grill in Watsonville. The restaurant was opened in July 1947 by her father and her uncles Clem and George "Blondie"— their cousin Pete (who came to the United States from Croatia when he was sixteen) later joined the partnership. Geri recalled that, when she was growing up, her parents were at the restaurant 90 percent of the time, and so her grandmother often babysat her, since she lived next door. Geri went to Mora High School.

> *My dad would get to work at 5:30 in the morning; breakfast was served at 6:00 a.m. His good friend Vic Ginelli, of Mity Nice Bakery, which was also on Main Street, came in every morning to philosophize with Dad. They baked really delicious fresh bread for us; people would come in and order our garlic bread just to take home. Then came the lunch and dinner shifts. Back then, "closing time" meant 2:00 a.m.*

Nick did all of the office work for the restaurant; as bookkeeper, he used an antique adding machine, the kind with a long lever attached. He also

Right: The Catalyst menu. Great food and large portions—always a busy kitchen, day and night. *Courtesy of the Santa Cruz Museum of Art and History (MAH).*

Below: Kathleen Manoff, Manoff's Rancho Burger. *Courtesy of Tom and Kathleen Manoff.*

Photograph of the outside of the Miramar Grill, a popular Croatian meeting spot in Watsonville. *Author's collection.*

had beautiful handwriting and kept all the account books tidy. Nick helped many people who had just arrived from Croatia file their immigration and citizenship papers. Some of the Croatian immigrants started as boarders at Geri's grandmother's place. Geri continued:

> *We used to get the vinegar for our salad dressing from a family in Morgan Hill; all of it homemade, and it was so good. We ordered our wine from the local Gallo Distributor in Watsonville. The dinner menu used to offer abalone—two big pieces for $3.75. The soldiers from Fort Ord in Monterey often came in to eat while on leave; then to visit the "red-light district" further down on Main Street. Watsonville used to be known as "Sin City!"*

Geri has fond memories of the Fourth of July parades, since they took place on Main Street, directly in front of the restaurant.

> *Oh, the parades were so much fun—we brought the bar stools and chairs out on the sidewalks, served sandwiches and drinks, beer, et cetera. Although, after a few years, that all changed. In the 1960s, there was a fire next door,*

and we were able to buy that parcel and make it into a banquet room, and we built an extension on the kitchen. After the 1989 earthquake, the whole town of Watsonville suffered; the buildings next door were boarded up for a really long time, and all of the repairs were so expensive.

Geri also has a few great stories about the celebrities who dined at the Miramar.

It was around 1958, when Alfred Hitchcock was filming the movie Vertigo *down in San Juan Bautista. Kim Novak stayed just across the street at the Resetar Hotel and came in for dinner. Then, in 1988, Loni Anderson and Joe Penny starred in a made-for-TV mystery called* Whisper Kill. *Dad was an extra in that—he was supposed to sit at the bar and drink coffee. The film crew and production team had to have everything catered, because they had a strict union rule—but they didn't know our restaurant was always union, so they missed out on the best homemade food! My dad "retired" at age eighty-four, but still came in to eat and say hello to the customers. The people who worked at our place were really special; to name a few: Virginia, Judy, Edna and Rosemary. Such wonderful and fond memories.*

Virginia Poulos said:

I worked as a waitress at the Miramar Bar and Grill on Main Street in Watsonville—I was there for thirty-five years! A lot of people considered the Miramar their favorite place for dinner. They had breaded veal cutlets and served pasta with a red sauce and brown gravy mixed together— Slavonian style. Parents let their kids "pay the bill" to the host Blondie, who handed them a lollipop. Businesses just signed their tabs and got billed once a month; everything was so old-fashioned.

After fifty-one years in business, the Miramar Bar and Grill closed in 1998.

Malio's on the Santa Cruz Wharf was very popular with both the locals and the tourist crowd; it was a place where diners could count on getting the freshest fish, order all-you-can-eat spaghetti and get a big welcome from the owner, Malio J. Stagnaro. The restaurant opened in 1965 in the center of the wharf, with a menu that offered patrons thirty-five varieties of seafood. Robert Canepa was the head chef. Behind the bar was a large,

(C) PAJARO VALLEY HISTORICAL ASSOCIATION 2009.0.782B

Pete and Emily Derpich at the Miramar Grill, Watsonville. *Courtesy of the Pajaro Valley Historical Association.*

colorful mural that was painted on wood and depicted scenes of old Santa Cruz and fishermen and boats. The best story about the mural, of course, comes straight from Malio himself. Quoting from Elizabeth Spedding Calciano's interview with him conducted in 1972, it is reprinted here with permission from the Regional History Project, UCSC.

Calciano: How did you happen to decide to do the mural? It's certainly a conversation piece.

Stagnaro: Well, Elizabeth, I wanted something different than a mirror in there, 'cause I think people get drunk, start looking at themselves in the mirror, and you get looking funny, and you start looking older, and you start looking uglier, and I've been through some of these stages myself, and I wanted something different. And I talked with the architects, Stevens and Calender, architects, and they had a boy in there at that time, and he was trying to become an AIA you know...he was finishing up, you see, before he could become an AIA, and he says, "Well Malio, how about a mural?" I says, "By golly, that's good thinking. And if we do, I'd like to come up with the characters of the wharf." So in looking around, I go to San Francisco, I ran into these boys, and by golly, Elizabeth, if they weren't from Santa Cruz originally.

Calciano: The ones who…

Stagnaro: The Redmond boys. And right away I walked in, and I kind of forgot the name, I never put these things together, and he says, "You're Mr. Stagnaro from Santa Cruz. My father was a very close friend of yours." And they did the mural for us. So the former Santa Cruz boys went to school with my nephews and went to high school with my nephews and nieces, and their father was a painter, a house painter, and was a great friend of mine.

Calciano: That's great. So they already had an idea of some of the wharf people.

Stagnaro: So I told them how I wanted them with the mustache, and they made a lot of drawings and finally came up with what I wanted. And I had some old time postcards, some old postcards of the Casino, of the Leibbrandt-Miller Bathhouse, which is the forerunner to the Casino; and the old Sea Beach Hotel that I knew as a boy, and we had the davits and came up with something very nice.

Calciano: You pretty much specified what you wanted.

Stagnaro: Oh I specified what I wanted, yes. Then you see the trademark, which is myself on my brother's shoulders, that was an old original picture.

Mural hanging in Malio's on the Wharf (currently hanging inside Gilda's). "Located on the picturesque Santa Cruz Municipal Wharf, with a 150-foot window that overlooks the beautiful Monterey Bay and coastline. Open daily from 11:00 a.m. to 11:00 p.m." *Photograph by author.*

While driving south on Highway 1, toward Watsonville, one could find a really great restaurant just off the side of the highway. Sometimes restaurants are discovered by simple word-of-mouth recommendations, and sometimes, they are found by pure luck. Carolyn Swift recalls:

> *At the Rob Roy Junction where Freedom Boulevard meets Highway 1, near Aptos High School was the Mon Desir Dining Inn. It was owned for a time by Edna Messini and her husband, Ray, from 1962 to 1964. They later ran the Venetian Court in Capitola and were, for many years, involved in the Capitola Begonia Festival.*

Matchbook from Mon Desir Dining Inn, Aptos. "Featured in the cocktail lounge is George Weales on piano, playing your favorite requests." *Author's collection.*

The Bayview Hotel in Aptos Village was built by Jose Arano in 1878 and is therefore regarded as the oldest hotel in Santa Cruz County. The hotel has a distinctive mansard roof and four marble fireplaces; it is also listed as a State Historical Monument (E Clampus Vitus #WM51VQ) as well as being in the National Register of Historic Places in Santa Cruz County, #92000259. Carolyn Swift said, "The Bayview Hotel has such a great location, and it deserves dedicated attention. The restaurant has been reinvented a number of times."

Mary's Tamale Parlor was Carolyn's favorite Watsonville family restaurant. She said, "It was located in an old house on Freedom Boulevard, and they served 'real Spanish food.' Later, it became Zuniga's, the name of the family owners. It finally moved to the Watsonville Airport. Their recipe for enchiladas never varied, and were even sold in packages at Deluxe Foods in Aptos."

The Del Monte Cafe in Watsonville was the classic combination of a top-notch restaurant and favorite watering hole. It was located near the Southern Pacific Railroad Station on the corner of Walker and Beach Streets, and it was owned and operated by the Kovacich family from the 1960s to the 1990s. It is remembered for its consistently delicious food and its old-fashioned customer service.

Early 1960s postcard from the Bayview Hotel, Aptos. *Courtesy of Norman Davis.*

Left: Telephone book advertisement for Mary's Tamale Parlor, Watsonville. *Author's collection.*

Right: Menu from the Del Monte Cafe, Watsonville. *Courtesy of the Pajaro Valley Historical Association.*

POPULAR DRINKS OF THE 1960s

Champagne Cocktail: In a Champagne flute, carefully drop two dashes of bitters on one sugar cube placed in the bottom of the flute, add one ice cube, fill the flute with Champagne, garnish with a lemon rind spiral.

When pouring the Champagne, tilt the glass, so that the effervescence lasts. This is a cocktail with a mesmerizing show for the customer who ordered it. Considered a festive holiday drink.

Matchbooks from Malio's, Facelli's and Zanze's Rocky Falls. Cocktails prepared by author. Photograph by author. *Author's collection.*

Martinez: In a cocktail shaker filled with ice, pour one ounce of Gin, one ounce of dry Vermouth, one-quarter of a teaspoon of Curacao, dash of orange bitters; shake and strain into a V-shaped Martini glass; garnish with an orange slice and a cherry.

The bartender Jerry Thomas is credited with this recipe while working at the Occidental Hotel in San Francisco in the nineteenth century. In 1862, he wrote an important book on drinks and drink recipes—the first of its kind published in America—called The bar-tenders guide: a complete cyclopedia of plain and fancy drinks; containing clear and reliable directions for mixing all the beverages used in the United States.

Whiskey Sour: In a cocktail shaker filled with ice, pour two ounces of Rye Whiskey, squeeze one-half of a lemon and add one-half of a teaspoon of powdered sugar; shake and strain into a Sour glass; garnish with a half wheel of lemon.

A variation called a New York Sour can be made by floating a bar spoon of red wine on top.

Chapter 4

The 1970s

NATURAL FOODS AND RECYCLING

At the beginning of the 1970s, the Census recorded that Santa Cruz County's population had grown to 123,790 people, which was almost double what it had been in the 1950s. The area has always been attractive due to its temperate climate and fresh air. It was during these years that many people wanted to escape from the urban sprawl, smog and air pollution of the city. Moving to the redwoods, and a local beach culture of surfing and "taking it easy," seemed like a perfect choice. Suddenly, there was an increase in the number of restaurants that served natural foods. The owners advertised on signage and in menus that their chefs cooked with only fresh and organic ingredients. In the 1970s, people found that these restaurants reflected their own philosophies about eating unadulterated and unprocessed foods; they could enjoy eating out while celebrating a healthy lifestyle.

Earth Day was born on April 22, 1970, and recycling went from an idea and something that everyone did at home to something that everyone could do at work, too. Something as basic as flattening out cardboard boxes became a routine chore for busboys at night. Elementary and junior high schools were designated as recycle centers and drop-off places for Santa Cruz citizens. Then, reclamation centers for business and commercial drop-off were finally built after years of public input, and the city and county hired more employees to handle the larger workload. There was steady growth in UCSC's enrollment; starting in the fall of 1970, the number of students enrolled was 3,713 (including graduate students), and by June 1979, that number had grown to 5,953.

Nature's Harvest was a popular vegetarian restaurant that was in a good location for the people who lived in mid-county, just past Twin Lakes State Beach. Next door to Nature's Harvest was the famous Buckharts's Candy Kitchen, and there was also a macramé shop nearby. Ellen McCarthy worked as a waitress at Nature's Harvest from 1971 to 1974; she was also in charge of making the made-to-order salads. McCarthy said:

> The food was simple, but the preparation and flavors were a revelation. I drove my 1964 Volkswagen Beetle to work every day. The tables were huge repurposed cable spools cut low to the ground, and people just sat down on big cushions. I had to learn to serve while wearing a short skirt—sort of a bend and swoop, then carefully put the plates down. One of the most asked-for dishes was mushroom stroganoff with roasted cashews. There was a fantastic organic apple pie that was made every day.

Nature's Harvest was only licensed for beer and wine. It is remembered as a place where young people went to eat with their friends and listen to live folk music on Fridays, Saturdays and Sundays (with no cover charge). The

Nature's Harvest menu from the mid-1970s. *Author's collection.*

31—Help Wanted

High Street LOCAL

Applications will be accepted beginning Feb. 16 afternoon. Positions available
for dudes & tomatoes over
21. Restaurant type em-
ployment.

Long hair, hippy
types DESIRABLE
224 Cardiff Place
(off High Street)

Is Live Boogie

Telephone book advertisement for
High Street Local. *Author's collection.*

owner, Marion Wieland, went on to teach cooking classes on local cable television channel 8, Capitola TV.

The High Street Local was located on Cardiff Place, which was just off of High Street near the UCSC campus. It was a small restaurant, and it wasn't in business for very long, but it was a popular meeting place for students. As the restaurant's help wanted ad said: "Long hair, hippy types desirable."

Ted Burke has been the owner of the spectacular Shadowbrook Restaurant in Capitola since 1972, along with his business partner, Bob Munsey. Ted described how the Shadowbrook adapted to recycling in the 1970s. He said, "The City of Capitola has always been at the forefront (since we're so close to the Soquel Creek and the Pacific Ocean) of progressive policy. Our restaurant welcomed recycling early on. It was the natural thing to do." Shadowbrook's patrons enter the restaurant by going down in a unique cable car, where they can look out of the windows and view the beautiful Soquel Creek below.

Ted described how he got into the restaurant scene. "You've heard of the expression 'A Year or a Career'? It means you know after a year of doing it that it's either a calling or that you're meant to do something else." He recalls hearing a political strategist say, "When reviewing job applications, anyone who has experience in restaurants gets moved up to the top of the pile. That's because they're used to working as a team, can think on their feet, show an economy of movement and are proven problem-solvers. A lot of people actually started out here with us at the Shadowbrook and then, after a while, went on to open up their own restaurant."

On September 14, 1982, the City of Santa Cruz passed a resolution supporting the "Can and Bottle Recycling Initiative." This new law required a minimum five-cent deposit on all beer and soft drink containers sold in the state; the ultimate goal of this law was for citizens and businesses, including restaurants, to reduce litter and solid waste. This decision was made because the initiative was supported by 80 percent of all Californians, and it had been endorsed by over four hundred organizations statewide.

Carol Champion worked in the UCSC library for thirty-two years. She remembers enjoying the Downtowner on Cathcart, a side street off Pacific Avenue. She recalled:

It was a great place for substantial home-cooked meals. El Azteca had really good Mexican food. The owner and cook used to work at Manny Santana's place [Manuel's] *in Aptos. As a child, I wanted to eat at Zanze's off Highway 17, going north, close to Scotts Valley. It looked so exotic, but it closed before I was old enough to go there on my own. From age thirteen to twenty, I worked at the Ben Lomond drug store that had the Village Fountain. Connie Armstrong and her husband were the owners. It later was sold to Rexall Drugs, and the fountain disappeared. I liked working at the Fountain. Connie was my first boss. She had previously been a buyer for a prominent clothing company in New York. She was a very intelligent, sophisticated and kind person. She sat me down on my first day of work—I was only a teenager—and taught me the rudiments of work life. I am truly very grateful to her. She was a wonderful role model as well as a practical teacher. I learned how to cook on a grill and make milkshakes and fountain cokes.*

Joe Hall worked for the City of Santa Cruz Planning Department and Redevelopment Agency. He said:

In the 1970s, the health inspection laws and policies for restaurants went through major changes, becoming much more rigid than in previous years. There were now standardized health and safety rules for grease traps, drains and sewer lines, plus much stricter fire department requirements. Permits were more expensive and the process for buying a liquor license more complicated than ever—in order to avoid a concentration of liquor stores.

Joe remembered his favorite restaurant during these years. "We used to really enjoy having dinner at Castagnola's, where it was literally a 'Who's Who' of Santa Cruz."

Al McLean said, "Castagnola's was probably the quietest restaurant, sound-wise, in town. They were in direct competition with the Colonial Inn for meeting up with someone for an important business deal. It was pretty pricey, even for lunch, but their food was excellent." On Friday nights, the restaurant listed a special bouillabaisse on the menu. Joanne Le Boeuf remembers going to Castagnola's. "The waiters stood and made your

Grace, Talent, Beauty, and Taste.

Castagnola's
"A MATTER OF TASTE"
Continental dining in the downtown Santa Cruz Park Plaza. Phone 426-4222.

Castagnola's advertisement in a Miss California Pageant program from 1979. "Continental dining in the downtown Santa Cruz Park Plaza." *Author's collection.*

Caesar salad right there at your table; it was very posh and elaborate." Jill Castagnola was only a little girl when Castagnola's was all the rage, but she said that she remembers it was "so elegant." Her father, Al Castagnola, was in the service in World War II and met her mother at Locatelli's (now Scopazzi's) in Boulder Creek.

Cindy Lepore-Hart owned and operated Seychelle's from 1978 to 1991, which featured organic Mediterranean cuisine. It was one of the first—if not the first—restaurants that offered a farm-to-table dining experience in Santa Cruz. Cindy cooked everything from scratch with locally grown vegetables and herbs, and she used recipes that reflected her Italian heritage. Seychelle's had once been located in the courtyard behind Bookshop Santa Cruz and across the way from Kelly's Bakery but moved to its final location on Cedar Street. Cindy recalled:

> *Storage space was always tight in the old place. I had to go up and down a ladder to get supplies in the loft; it was always so cramped. We found an old house on Cedar Street with a nice glassed-in front porch and a huge garden. I set up and designed the new kitchen all by myself, and laid the black and white tile floor by myself. I had a walk-in refrigerator built on the side of the building. There was an old clawfoot bathtub in the bathroom—original to the house—and on opening night, since I had been up since dawn, I decided to take a bubble bath and have a glass of Champagne! Everything on the menu was homemade, with our specialty being fresh pasta made-to-order. There were always lots of big pots of boiling water on the stove. I also made our own hibiscus lemonade.*

Cindy Lepore-Hart working in her kitchen at Seychelle's. In addition to her freshly made pastas, the menu also listed a hummus platter and Cindy's homemade dolmas. *Courtesy of Cindy Lepore-Hart.*

Cindy also had a large wooden drying rack built up high on the kitchen wall for hanging all the day's different pastas. She recalls wine reps would visit and make suggestions, pairing her pasta dishes with a J. Lohr or an Ahlgren wine from California. During the off-season months, Cindy sold her fresh salad dressings in local markets and wrote chapters for her cookbook called *The Eclectic Noodle.* Cindy was also the founder of the popular Santa Cruz Pasta Festival. After a trip to Venice, Italy, Cindy came back with a recipe for black pasta made with squid ink, and it quickly sold out at the festival. Cindy said, "A lot of downtown restaurants closed because of the earthquake, including mine, but I loved the experience of owning my own place." Cindy and her family still live in Santa Cruz, where she is now a professional videographer and photographer.

In early March 2019, Paul and Charlene Lee and Joanne Le Boeuf sat together in the Lees' spacious and comfortable living room and shared the memories they had of running the Wild Thyme Cafe. It was located downstairs in the old Cooper House on the Pacific Garden Mall; patrons entered by passing the Oakroom, which featured a giant taxidermy buffalo head, and the bathrooms before going down a set of narrow stairs. Paul said he chose the name "because of its play on words; the herb thyme correlates to the Thymus gland and highlights the importance of it being the center of the immune system." Joanne, who was the head chef, recalls:

Specialties of the house were sole almondine, shrimp crêpes with dill and cream sauce, chicken with juniper berries and boeuf bourguignonne. We ordered our fish fresh from Stagnaro Bros. Seafood, Inc. Most of the recipes came from cookbooks by Dionne Lucas and Julia Child, but I expanded and tweaked them a little. Another specialty was sweetbreads with thyme (Paul's favorite).

Paul bought most of the wine from the Liquor Barn on Morrissey Boulevard. Both Joanne and Charlene delighted in remembering their freshly made desserts, like crème caramel and chocolate custard mousse. Joanne laughed and said, "Basically, we were rank amateurs, all of us were so highly educated—and every day, it was such hard work; although, we certainly had a great time." Charlene's dear friend and local artist Eloise Smith designed the restaurant's interior, chose and hung all of the artwork on the walls and helped out in the kitchen. "Eloise always generated a sense of hilarity and *bons temps*." The building's owner was Max Walden, who had years of previous experience with restaurants at the same location. Paul said, "We invited musicians from UCSC to perform for the dinner crowd; it was really fantastic hearing a classical string trio live, and the patrons enjoyed it too."

Paul's dear friend Page Smith was the celebrated maître d'. Paul said, "Page would wear his fanciest blazer and Gary Cooper's loafers [which he had bought at auction] and enjoyed handing out menus to the patrons and pouring coffee." The restaurant's exterior sign was painted by Don Cochrane. The menu was a large hand-printed broadside that was personally designed and printed by the great American printer Jack Stauffacher, another great friend of Paul's. After working fourteen-hour days and knowing that restaurant work was not her *raison d'être*, Joanne went back to college. In 1975, after a good run of about nine months, Paul decided that it was time to close.

The Cooper House, located on the corner of Pacific Avenue and Cooper Street, was known for being the "Heart and Soul" of the Pacific Garden Mall. In front was a large courtyard that was full of tables and chairs, called the Sidewalk Cafe. People flocked to sit, listen and dance to the jazz band Warmth, which was led by Don McCaslin. They played music on an outdoor stage in the afternoons and evenings, often five days a week.

In addition to the Wild Thyme Cafe, there were many trendy shops inside the Cooper House that sold candles, jewelry and fancy chocolates.

COOPERHOUSE

SHELLFISH

Steamed
Pacific Hardshell Clams 3⁶⁵
Mussels 3⁶⁵

Sauteed
with mushrooms & white wine
Scallops 3⁹⁵
Dungeness Crab 4²⁵
Oysters 4²⁵

Sauteed Provencale
in garlic-tomato-sweet basil
Scallops 3⁷⁵
Dungeness Crab 3⁷⁵
Oysters 3⁷⁵

Cocktails
Shrimp 2⁷⁵
Dungeness Crab 3²⁵
Sevici Scallop 3²⁵
    (marinated in lime juice, hot
    chilis, onions and herbs)

Louis Salad
Shrimp 3⁹⁵
Crab 4⁶⁵

6% sales Tax on all service

Hot Loaf Sandwiches
with Remoulade sauce

Oyster 2⁹⁵
Shrimp 2⁶⁵
Scallops 2⁷⁵
Dungeness Crab 2⁷⁵

Cold Loaf Sandwiches
(marinated in garlic olive oil,
tarragon vinegar and herbs)
Crab 2⁷⁵
Shrimp 2⁶⁵

Avacado Boats
with Caviar Dressing
Shrimp 3²⁵
Crab 3⁷⁵

★ ★ ★ ★ ★ ★ ★ ★ ★ ★ ★ ★ ★ ★ ★

Hamburger 2⁴⁵
Cheeseburger 2⁶³
French Fries .... .75
Clam Chowder . .75 cup 1⁰⁰ bowl
Dinner Salad 1⁰⁰
Marinated Fruit Salad 1²⁵
Large Fruit Salad 2⁹⁵
Vegetable of the Day 1⁰⁰
Rice .... .50

Above: Wild Thyme Cafe sign. The sign is five feet wide and one and a half feet tall. *Photograph by author. Courtesy of Dr. Paul A. Lee.*

Left: Cooper House menu from the mid-1970s. The verso side of the menu features the Cooper House's wine list, with selections from Mondavi, Kenwood and Mirassou vineyards, plus a Bargetto champagne. *Author's collection.*

It was once home to The Crêpe Place, and for a while, the building's owner and entrepreneur, Max Walden, ran his own restaurant there called Maximilliano's. Max commissioned the spectacular and very large stained-glass dome, which was created by Bonny Doon Art Glass. The menu included an extensive wine list. After the 1989 earthquake, the building was condemned, and crowds of people (including the author) stood watching as a wrecking ball slammed into the building's brick façade.

Dr. Paul A. Lee described how he came to be a part owner of the Whole Earth Restaurant:

> *Reverend Herb Schmidt, Jerry Lasko and I started a nonprofit called the University Services Agency, and we started the restaurant in 1970. Really, it was to offer people—both students and faculty—an alternative to cafeteria food. It was the first time that an organic garden on a University of California campus was considered an active purveyor for a restaurant. The Alan Chadwick Garden had been started in 1967, and we saw it to be the perfect resource of fresh, organic vegetables for the restaurant. We hired Sharon Cadwallader as our chef, and we had the big deck built with tables and benches; it was such a perfect congregating place under the redwoods. The party for the opening was really a lot of fun; the Red Mountain Boys* [including Page Stegner and Jim Houston] *came and played bluegrass music, and everyone danced until the early morning.*

Stewart Brand, founder of the *Whole Earth Catalog*, came to the opening of the Whole Earth Restaurant and gave an inaugural speech. He sketched out the coming decade as a time when there would be a rise of hippie entrepreneurs, and he predicted that money wouldn't be the object but instead creative thinking would advance the economy. Dr. Paul A. Lee has written about his experience with Alan Chadwick in his 2013 book *There Is a Garden in the Mind, A Memoir of Alan Chadwick and the Organic Movement in California*. In it, he wrote:

> *The story is of the development of the garden at UCSC and the subsequent gardens he developed after he left the university, promoting organic procedures in food and flower production, with his special method and system, the French Intensive and Biodynamic, wherever he went. He is credited with inaugurating the organic movement in California, and his influence was remarkable, reaching all the way to the new California cuisine.*

Map of Santa Cruz in 1974. *Author's collection.*

Al McLean also remembers the Broken Egg Omelet House. "It was a great breakfast place, because you could get eggs any which way you could imagine, and they served great coffee. I loved their scrambled eggs because they mixed in lots of mushrooms, and the country fries had just the right amount of onions and chives. It closed when the corner parking garage was built."

The original Tampico Kitchen and Lounge was located across from the Boardwalk and was opened in November 1955 by Julio and Otila Gomez. Marion Dale Pokriots recalls, "We liked to go to the Tampico Kitchen down near the Boardwalk on Friday nights. Then, we'd go to the library [at the time, it was open until 9:00 p.m.] and pick up an armload of books and read for the rest of the evening." Marion is a historian, editor and writer of many books about the local history of Santa Cruz County. Carol Kirchner also said, "Tampico's used to be my parents' favorite place!"

Otila Gomez cooked, waitressed and washed dishes when the restaurant first opened. The couple started out with four tables and five stools; one day, they only made fifty-five cents by selling one tamale and a pack of gum. Then, in December 1955, the flood hit Santa Cruz and Tampico's was in shambles. But the Gomezes were determined and didn't give up.

Above: Broken Egg Omelet House. *Author's collection.*

Left: Tampico Kitchen and Lounge matchbook. Located on lower Pacific Avenue, this was a popular place for happy hour, which featured their delicious in-house margaritas. *Courtesy of Norman Davis.*

They worked even harder, and in 1961, they moved their business to Pacific Avenue. In 1973, they opened Little Tampico in Soquel, which featured a beautiful creekside view. At one time, the Gomezes also owned and operated Tampico Grande (formerly Costella's Chalet) in Felton.

Judy Steen recalled, "L'Oustalou was a really fun place to go—there was a long table down the middle section filled with plates of hors d'oeuvres, and everyone helped themselves until their entrée was served." Suzanne Grelson Rom owned and operated L'Oustalou from 1973 to 1985. Suzanne remembered, "I'd go to Shopper's Corner every morning to buy all my vegetables and look over their meat selection. Always trusted their meats. The fish people would come by to the restaurant in the morning too. There wasn't a lot of storage space, so the wine was chosen and used up pretty quickly."

Suzanne said:

> I started in just the lunch trade, and then, business grew by word of mouth, so we opened for dinner. Setting up the recycling was fairly easy— we separated the bottles and cans. There were even people that came by to take away the extra produce, carrot tops, et cetera, for their backyard compost. Everyone became terribly aware of the amount of pollution in the ocean. We regularly hired Pete's Outflow to come and professionally clean out the grease trap. There was always local artwork on the walls, like Hardy Hansen. The employees were often students at UCSC, and there was always lots of UCSC faculty who were regular customers, like Page and Eloise Smith and Paul and Charlene Lee.

Suzanne said, "One of the best things I ever did was to hire a local writer, Peter Beagle." His most famous book was *The Last Unicorn*, which was published in 1968. Suzanne continued:

> Peter came to play his guitar and sing French folk songs during Saturday evening dinners. Peter attracted many famous and not-so-famous people: Richard Chamberlain, Eugene Ionesco, Peter Donat and many writers, artists, actors and producers. It was fun, and of course, there are many stories to tell. And as for favorite memories, it really boiled down to all the times spent working with a wonderful staff and then finishing a great year by holding our special Holiday and New Year's dinner, when we served entrées such as suckling pig and roast goose—with all the trimmings. Peter always sang at these dinners, and once our patrons had left, we all sat down

and shared a meal. I then closed the restaurant for a month and went back to New England to relax and refresh and plan for the next exciting year.

On Wednesday nights, the visiting chef was often Michelangelo Rosato, who cooked manicotti, linguine bolognese and the popular chicken San Lorenzo (a recipe invented by Suzanne). Here is the description of chicken San Lorenzo, as listed on a menu: chicken breast poached in chicken broth, covered with white sauce, then breaded and sautéed and covered with Michelangelo's Neapolitan tomato sauce.

Jozseph Schultz has had a massive influence on the food scene in Santa Cruz; he opened his restaurant, India Joze, in 1972 and, at one time, employed eighty people at the Center Street location. It continued to be relevant and groundbreaking until it closed in 1999. Schultz said: "I'm like a food evangelist, because I really believe in making everything better." He described what it was like when he started out in the early 1970s. "I regularly went up to San Francisco to stock up on everything—I found a lot of wonderful and strange herbs and spices there in Chinatown. I didn't

L'Oustalou's Christmas dinner menu. *Courtesy of Suzanne Grelson Rom.*

have a real plan for the restaurant at first; I made things up as I went along, developing cooking techniques, using my instincts. I have always had a passion for learning about the world." Christina Waters said, "India Joze was in its golden age, serving multi-ethnic foods of amazing complexity and ingenious spicing. Schultz would travel to refresh his idea arsenal and then come back and dazzle everyone." Melody Sharp recalled when she first started going to India Joze. "I learned a lot about new tastes and flavors there—always so surprising!" The Calamari Festival brought Jozseph national recognition and was celebrated for seventeen years. Jozseph said, "It was a real windfall—sort of a super cheap enterprise, and everything about it was fun!" One of the festival's many witty print ads invited potential India Joze customers to "Take a Wok on the Wild Side!" Jozseph's approach to cooking inspired a generation of foodies in Santa Cruz.

Jay's restaurant was located on the corner of Water and Ocean Streets. Nancy Karr Sharmer said:

My husband Jay and I owned Jay's from 1970 to 1973. The thing I remember most was all the cops and firemen coming in, which is how Jay ended up in the SCPD [Santa Cruz Police Department]. *We would close down on Thanksgiving and Christmas and cook several turkeys and all the fixings, and the cops and firemen on duty would come in the back door and celebrate the holidays with us. I remember having to drive over to San Jose to pick up supplies when he found himself short on things. I also took care of the payroll but didn't work in the restaurant per se. I remember two uniforms at different times—I think one was tan and the other was red. We redid the entire inside, and all the booths and stools were red, so we changed to red uniforms.*

Jay started out as a dishwasher, then became a cook, then night manager, then manager, then bought it. I loved Jay's because of the wonderful friends we made with the cops and firemen coming there. It was like a second home for some of them. We also had CB radios back then, and the restaurant was known as "the Watering Hole," and Jay was "French Fry" and our son was "Little Spud." Jay's brother Joe, who worked there for a short time, was "Hash Brown." A lot of CB chatter going back and forth! After the earthquake, Jay stood for hours on the Soquel bridge directing everyone away from going over it because it was too damaged.

In 2011, the Santa Cruz Museum of Art and History (MAH) awarded one of its Historic Landmark Blue Plaques to The Lost Weekend restaurant

Jay's Restaurant on Ocean Street. Virgil, the cook, and Louie, the dishwasher, in the 1970s. *Courtesy of Nancy Karr Sharmer.*

and saloon in Bonny Doon. The Blue Plaques are awarded to structures in Santa Cruz County that are at least fifty years old and hold historic significance. Local historian Judy Steen researched the history of The Lost Weekend and said, "It started out in a building that was originally the Bonny Doon Cash Store. The store was opened in the 1920s by Louis 'Luigi' and Mary Iocapetti." Afterward, the building had a succession of owners. It transformed from a little neighborhood store that sold milk, bread, snacks, pizza and hamburgers into a tavern that sold beer and wine and had a pool table. It got its name from the famous 1945 film noir drama *The Lost Weekend*, starring Ray Milland. During the 1970s, when Frank Stacey ran the place, it even had a licensed card room. In 1983, Bonny Doon Vineyards took over and it became a destination tasting room for the popular wines of Randall Grahm. In 2008, it was sold to Jim Beauregard, who owns Shopper's Corner. Jim's son, Ryan, now manages the Beauregard Vineyards Tasting Room.

Many visitors to Santa Cruz over the years remember Garbini's, which was famous for its fine steaks and Italian cuisine. Carolyn Swift said, "I still remember the Garbini's radio ad from the 1970s. They'd play dour organ music, the announcer said, 'Sadness rains in the hearts of men. There is no joy...(more mournful notes)...for today is Wednesday, and Garbini's is closed.' Then, a sprightly tune, 'But don't worry, the restaurant will be open tomorrow!'"

Carolyn Swift said, "In Watsonville, there were Chinese restaurants that dotted Main Street, particularly 'Lower' Main, toward the Pajaro River. One of the most popular was the Chop Stick."

Christina Waters is a longtime local restaurant reviewer. She said:

> *In the mid- to late 1970s, from San Francisco to Santa Cruz, the dining craze was already in high gear. Pearl Alley Bistro was opened by Odette Emery and run by her daughter, Marilyn, and son-in-law, Eric Strayer. Eric was a big wine lover, and pretty soon, the authentic French cooking and the long wine list attracted winemakers and other serious foodies. Everybody went there and met up there.*

Garbini's postcard. "Where you have a choice of thirty-two entrées, including abalone steaks. Enjoy listening to Gloria Daye play the Hammond organ." *Author's collection.*

Chop Stick, Watsonville. Photograph dated 1972. *Courtesy of the Pajaro Valley Historical Association.*

The Pearl Alley Bistro was best known for its special fondue dinner, which was listed for either a single person or two to three people, and the recipe was a classic one—made with Gruyère and Swiss cheeses and white wine.

Christina continued:

> *Overlooking the Boardwalk, the Casablanca was another home of great cooking. Thanks to manager Billy Grippo, it had a deep and expansive wine cellar and hosted many winemaker dinners over the years. Castagnola's on River Street was essentially a glamorous drinking man's clubhouse with a restaurant attached. It had a suave maître d' who knew everyone. Pastas, steaks and cocktails. Very popular—especially with men after work and "ladies who lunched."*

Christina Waters is an adjunct professor in the Digital Arts and New Media Program at the University of California, Santa Cruz.

Chef Francis Tong was the manager of the New Riverside on Barson Street. Its building used to house the old Riverside Hotel and, therefore, still had a huge dining room, banquet room and kitchen. It was one of the first—if not the very first—restaurants in the Santa Cruz area to offer authentic northern

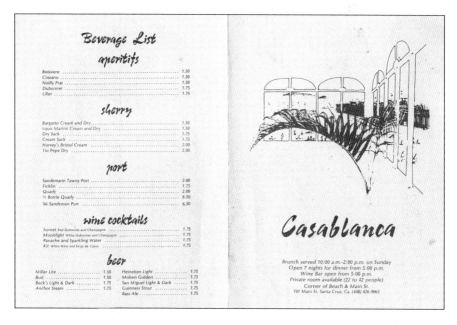

Casablanca menu. "Appetizers include marinated calamari and steamed clams. Entrées include broiled sole, veal marsala and chicken tarragon." Next door, there was also the Casablanca Motel. "A new, nicely furnished twenty-five-room motel with tile, glass-enclosed showers in apartments and panel-ray heat. All rooms face the Monterey Bay." *Author's collection.*

Chinese (Szechwan) food to its customers. New Riverside's banquet rooms were very much in demand; many community groups booked their meetings there—perhaps the restaurant's reputation for delicious authentic cuisine assured a full attendance. The master chef was Ming Chan Yuen, who brought decades of culinary experience with him. The restaurant's menu was extensive, with detailed descriptions of each dish. One restaurant reviewer described it as "one of the finest Szechwan Chinese restaurants in the Bay Area."

In the early 1970s and 1980s, Vester "Mother" Brown served homecooked Soul Food twice a month, from April to August, at the All Nations Church of God at Wilkes Circle, located on the West Side of Santa Cruz. Although her enterprise was not a restaurant by definition, for this book, she is represented as one of the very few African American chefs with a busy, working kitchen in Santa Cruz County.

Linda Wilshusen was one of the original employees at the Whole Earth Restaurant on the University of California, Santa Cruz campus. The restaurant was made famous by Sharon Cadwallader's and Judi Ohr's popular 1972 cookbook of the same name (Dr. Paul A. Lee wrote the introduction). Known for its organic and healthy food, the Whole Earth was the perfect place to incorporate fresh produce that was grown at The Alan Chadwick Garden. Linda said, "I learned to cook there—whatever was in season. I spent late nights washing dishes, met my husband there, too.

**MOTHER BROWN'S
Soul Food Dinners**

Saturday Oct. 14, 1978
Friendly Church of God in Christ
231 Wilkes Circle, Santa Cruz, CA
Time: 12 Noon Until
MENU: BBQ spare ribs, BBQ chicken, deep fried fish, BBQ links, mustard greens, baked beans, potato salad or baked beans, deep fried corn bread. Dessert (sold separately) Pies: lemon chiffon, coconut cream, sweet potatoes.
All regular Dinners $3.75
Combos $7.50
Around the World $9.00
Pies large $2.75   Small .70
Call 427-0285 or 427-1903 for free delivery on two or more orders.

Vester "Mother" Brown's Soul Food Kitchen advertisement from the *Santa Cruz Sentinel* on February 17, 1977. *Author's collection.*

My class schedule wove in nicely with my hours there, which was great. All of our bread was fresh and delivered by Staff of Life." When Linda served as president of the UCSC Alumni Association, she said she reconnected with a lot of her old classmates and fellow employees from the old days of working at the Whole Earth Restaurant. Linda loaned the author of this book a scanned photograph of her own copy of the *Whole Earth Cook Book*, which has a personal inscription to her written by Sharon. It says, "For Linda and all her love and laughter! I wish you a lifetime of sunshine x x."

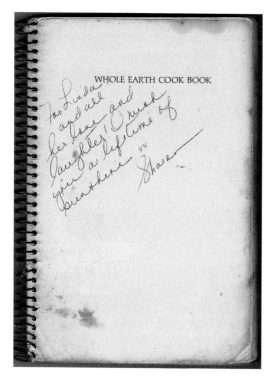

WHOLE EARTH COOK BOOK

Sharon Cadwallader's inscription
in *Whole Earth Cook Book. Courtesy of
Linda Wilshusen.*

POPULAR DRINKS OF THE 1970s

Bloody Mary Cocktail: In a Collins glass, pour two ounces of Vodka, three ounces of tomato juice, one-half of an ounce of lemon juice, one-half of a teaspoon of Worcestershire sauce, a pinch of salt, pepper and celery salt; stir well, then slowly fill with ice; garnish with a slim stalk of celery and wedge of lime.

This cocktail originated in the 1920s in Paris at Harry's New York Bar by its bartender, Ferdinand "Pete" Petiot. Soon after, he moved to New York City and began working at the King Cole Bar in the St. Regis Hotel, where he introduced the Bloody Mary to the American public.

Harvey Wallbanger: In a Collins glass filled with ice, pour two ounces of Vodka, three ounces of fresh orange juice; do not stir, carefully float one ounce of Galliano on top; garnish with an orange slice and a cherry.

This was a phenomenally popular drink in the 1970s, helped by its strange and ridiculous name. It was said to have been dreamed up by George Bednar, who was the marketing

Matchbooks from Miramar Fish Grotto, Pasatiempo Inn and Adolph's Italian Family Style Restaurant. *Cocktails prepared by author. Photograph by author. Author's collection.*

director for McKesson Imports Co. (the company that imported Galliano). Its amusing color poster, which was done in a pop art style, of a surfer riding a wave showed up "everywhere." It was conceived of and drawn by graphic artist Bill Young.

Frozen Strawberry Daiquiri: In an electric blender, pour two ounces of light Rum, one ounce of simple syrup, one ounce of fresh lime juice, one-half of a cup of frozen strawberries and one-half of a cup of crushed ice. Blend thoroughly and pour into a Margarita glass (chilled, if desired); garnish with a lime wheel.

Daiquiris were one of Ernest Hemingway's favorite cold drinks while he was living in Cuba. These Frozen Strawberry Daiquiris are often ordered by the pitcher and shared at the table.

Chapter 5

The 1980s

PART I
COMPUTERS AND EMAIL

In the 1980s, the Census recorded that the population of Santa Cruz County was 188,141 people. The incoming generation of eighteen-year-old UCSC students continued to change both the city and the county of Santa Cruz in many ways. The students' shopping styles affected not only the area's clothing stores, record shops and other merchants, but also the area's restaurants and coffeehouses. If a student lived off-campus, they shopped at both all-natural and conventional grocery stores in the neighborhood. The number of students enrolled at UCSC at the beginning of fall 1980 was 5,953 (including graduate students), and by June 1989, that number had grown to 9,456.

Restaurant menus from this period reflect the new lifestyle choices of ordering something "light" in calories. For instance, fried food took a back seat, and sushi was "in." Fresh and elaborate salads were also listed as main courses, and several restaurants set up expansive salad bars. A new term that was used to categorize people was "yuppies," or young, upwardly mobile professionals. A popular pastime for men and women in the 1980s was to join the local fitness gym and enroll in Jazzercise classes. Rollerblades were invented in 1983, and in-line skating became all the rage along the famous West Cliff Drive in Santa Cruz. It's a wide, flat sidewalk, a distance of two and a half miles going from the Dream Inn to the Natural Bridges State Beach, or a five-mile round trip. And on the other side are the big, beautiful homes facing the Pacific Ocean.

In the spring of 1986, the cult movie *Lost Boys*, directed by Joel Schumacher, was filmed in Santa Cruz and was released in 1987. The teenage vampire picture starred Kiefer Sutherland, Jason Patric, Corey Haim, Jami Gertz and Corey Feldman. The Pogonip Clubhouse was used as the location for Grandpa's house in the film. The Sea Cloud Restaurant, located on the Santa Cruz Municipal Wharf, was also used as the location where Lucy, played by Dianne Wiest, and Max, played by Edward Herrmann, meet for dinner. According to the local visitors' bureau, the Warner Bros. production brought in roughly $3 million to the Santa Cruz County area. This money was spent on dining and food, housing and hotel rooms, salaries and general services. Each season, the Santa Cruz Beach Boardwalk kicks off its Summer Movie Series with a free screening of *Lost Boys* at night on the sand—right where it all happened.

The personal computer has had a long-lasting impact on Santa Cruz County. First, it promised to help small businesses gain a perspective of income and expenses, and it was also especially good at handling inventory and personnel. In the 1980s, local restaurant owners and managers were eager to join the crowd; they wanted to purchase computer systems and set up their email accounts. Many people including purveyors described the effects that computers and email had on their lives and their businesses. Restaurant owners were also busy installing separate, dedicated telephone lines that were used to securely take credit card numbers—an immediate improvement over the old, manual imprint machines.

Ted Burke of the Shadowbrook restaurant said, "Starting in about 1978 or 1980, we figured the Shadowbrook would be the pioneers in bringing computers into our business. So, we bought a couple of Apple IIs, used those floppy discs and set up a new system of accounting and purchasing." Melody Sharp is a successful web designer based in Santa Cruz County. She said she moved from Southern California to Santa Cruz in 1981 to work as a tech writer. "I used to hang out at the old Computerland Mac store on Forty-First Avenue. It was frequented by a lot of gregarious, like-minded nerds—a kind of 'tribe' of early techies." Right from the start, Melody recognized the value of technology for small businesses. She said, "Suddenly, you could write emails, invoice and take orders at any time of day. This was so critical for marketing and reaching out to customers. Now that everything is on the web, it is essential for websites to be mobile-friendly." She also remembers eating at the old St. George Hotel. "Such beautiful décor; it was a very romantic setting."

John Tara of Stagnaro Bros. Seafood, Inc. described his company's adaptation to the computer and how it made his record keeping, purchases and inventory so much easier. He said, "The handwritten method of accounting was not keeping up with our business—for instance, today, I can immediately see what our customers' usage was yesterday or last week. I can even anticipate what they will need for next month, and that's the best way to stay on top of this business." Jozseph Schultz said, "The personal computer showed me where the cost margins were for both the perishable and non-perishable inventory. It made it easier since it was customizable, but I had the bookkeepers do it because I just wanted to cook!"

Jessie Durant, the archivist and historian at the Seaside Company, shared a couple of the many photographs of popular concessionaires at the Santa Cruz Beach Boardwalk that were taken during the 1980s. Over the years, thousands of local high school students landed their "first job" at the Boardwalk. It's hard work, but provides good training and learning skills, plus the experience looks great on a resume.

Catherine Faris was just twenty-six years old when she opened Trattoria Primitzia in Capitola, next door to Gayle's Bakery & Rotisserie. Catherine

Ottaviano Chachie and staff in the 1980s. Chachie's hot dogs were the classic choice for beachgoers. *Courtesy of the Seaside Company.*

Hodgie Wetzel working the order window at Hodgie's in the 1980s. Hodgie Wetzel helped organize the Brussels Sprouts Festival at the Boardwalk in 1981. *Courtesy of the Seaside Company.*

said, "The menu was 100 percent authentic Italian, and we served mostly Italian wines. It was unusual just for promoting that singular concept, but I had a clear vision of what I wanted to do." Due to strict zoning laws, Catherine said she had to win over her neighbors before she could open Trattoria Primitzia. "I went door to door, imploring the merchants in Capitola to accept my new business—I would be selling beer and wine, and I asked them to not oppose it." For the grand opening, Catherine sold tickets, and all of the night's proceeds were donated to the local food bank. She did a lot of research on limited partnership and drew up "shares" that people could then trade in for dinners. She said, "It really was an example of guerrilla marketing." It was such a successful idea that the "partners" became regulars and brought their friends. Catherine said the restaurant broke even after its first year. The *San Francisco Chronicle*, the *San Jose Mercury News* and other local newspapers raved about Primitzia. Patrons and loyal fans came several times a week. Catherine said:

> *I got my fresh fish from Race Street in San Jose delivered each morning.*
> *I ordered Italian specialty foods from Bay Area distributors, and I would*

meet them at a gas station to load the boxes in my car. I bought fancy, but used, pizza ovens. I had to plan really well because margins were always razor thin. There were millions of details. It was a lot of responsibility to meet payroll for fifty employees and pay the rent and all of the suppliers.

When her first child was born, Catherine went to work with him strapped in a front pack. She recalled, "I would reconcile the money from the night before, go to the bank, come back and peel shrimp, et cetera, go home and hand the baby over to my husband, Brian. Then, I'd change, come back and work the front of the house." After three kids and five years of working full time at the restaurant, Catherine wanted more time with her family and sold the restaurant. Catherine and her husband live part of the year in Puglia, Italy, where they lead group wine and food tours and run an olive oil export business called Pascarosa.

Bar managers agree that acquiring a computer really helped with the handling of liquor inventory. They could easily see what sold and what didn't sell, and they could see if seasonal promotions (like banners, table tents and coasters) helped sales. In the 1980s, the liquor industry began to seriously address the issue of driving under the influence (DUI). The phrase "designated driver" was frequently discussed in bartending trade magazines. Blood alcohol levels, drunk driving, liability and warnings about over-pouring remain real issues for bartenders and restaurant owners today.

Around the 1980s, larger establishments and hotels—particularly the venues that held conventions—installed automatic dispensers designed to pour an exact measured amount of alcohol. For years, soda drinks had already been dispensed this way to keep costs down. This new "bar gun" put a real cramp into the bartenders' training and personal style that was otherwise known as "eyeballing the ounce" or pouring a jigger and a half. But managers found that the automatic dispensers helped them to stay competitive and, in some cases, meant the survival of their business. They also stepped up their advertising with catchy print ads for "Lite Beer," including hanging up neon signs in the windows. Restaurants in the 1980s started to list non-alcoholic drinks on the menu. Of course, most popular drinks can be served without liquor. For example, the Orange Fizz is a simply a Collins glass full of ice with ginger ale and a splash of orange juice.

Mike Ferry is a senior planner with the City of Santa Cruz. He described the process involved with obtaining a liquor license in the city.

The city has a rigorous definition of low-risk and high-risk outlets; restaurants located in the county apply directly through the state— California Department of Alcoholic Beverage Control. Within city limits, however, the applicant discovers there are ordinances, which involve a close inspection of the facility, including its hours of operation, seating, menu and the kinds of liquor and food that will be served. An Administrative Use Permit is required to be approved at a public hearing with close supervision of the Police Department, which often takes three months to process. There are only so many liquor licenses allowed within the city limits, and there are strict ordinances for hours of operation due to police response and the issues of traffic and noise at night.

Sandi Imperio is the reference librarian at the Aptos and La Selva Beach branches of the Santa Cruz Public Library. She said:

There are a few Japanese restaurants in Watsonville [South County]. The Miyuki has been open the longest—since the early 1980s. It is on East Lake Avenue and is in a converted gas station. Needless to say, it's a little, dinky place, but they refer to it as "cozy." For the longest time, it was the only sushi, Japanese place in town. They used to have a buffet for lunch that was great. Years ago, when I worked for the Watsonville Public Library, a couple of coworkers and I used to go there for lunch once a month.

The Miyuki is still there on East Lake Avenue in Watsonville.

Chez Renee was located in Aptos and is remembered for its French cuisine, considered one of the best of its kind in Northern California. It was owned and operated by Jack and Renee Chyle from 1983 to 2000. Both are classically trained, and both graduated from the California Culinary Academy in San Francisco. Jack was always an early bird at the farmers' markets, buying fresh local fruits and vegetables. The grocers knew him well, and they set aside their very best just for him. The gourmet menu included smoked salmon, fresh duckling, a Grand Marnier soufflé and an extensive wine list. The restaurant won a 1988 *Wine Spectator* Award for Excellence.

Carol Kirchner is a second-generation native of Santa Cruz and went to Harbor High School. She was sixteen years old when she began working part time at The Plaza Bakery. Her sisters had also worked there, and she remembers making "mud cookies" in her backyard as a child. There was a baker named Lyle who made delicious orange rolls for The Plaza Bakery, and Carol believes that he also made them for the Shadowbrook. She said,

Menu from Miyuki, Watsonville. *Courtesy of the Pajaro Valley Historical Association.*

"At Christmas time, The Plaza Bakery carried special bar cookies, and we would put them in those pink boxes—lots of regular customers called in to order in advance. I enjoyed my job and was an expert on the bread-slicer machine."

During the big storm of 1982, all of the power went out, but Carol said, "My boss, Eugene Tartaglino, kept the bakery open. We served hot coffee and gave out every last thing in the shop." Carol worked at the bakery for seven years. Joanne Le Boeuf fondly remembers ordering the bakery's "delicious Amaretto cookies and Italian almond cake." Leo Stefani recalled, "During World War II, Mario Tartaglino had a standing order for doughnuts for all of Fort Ord, the cake kind made with lard—they were always fantastic!" In 1989, the Loma Prieta earthquake destroyed the entire Flatiron building, including The Plaza Bakery.

In the early 1980s, Carmen Kubas started out as a hostess at Adolph's, answering the phone and handling the takeout orders. She said, "You had to really be focused to deal with all of the checks and credit card receipts; there were so many interruptions and distractions! The skill sets of working in a restaurant are similar to those in sports. The aspects of working as a team are all there: the planning, reliance on others, focus and dedication, pride and feeling of accomplishment." Carmen believes that working in a restaurant is an important vocation. Currently, Carmen is the culinary teacher at King Kekaulike High School in Maui, Hawaii.

The Plaza Bakery after the 1989 earthquake. *Courtesy of Norman Davis.*

LUNCH

Luncheon — Served with Tureen of Soup or Salad & Ravioli or Spaghetti & Vegetables & Coffee

A La Carte — Served with Tureen of Soup or Salad & Vegetables

Special — Served with Salad or Cup of Soup or Vegetable or Pasta or French Fries

DAILY ENTREE
ROAST BEEF — SKIRT STEAK — GROUND CHUCK
COUNTRY FRIED STEAK — HAM

	LUNCHEON	ALA CARTE	SPECIAL
ENTREE OF THE DAY	$2.25	$1.95	$.175
ask your waitress for other entrees			
SKIRT STEAK		2.35	2.10	1.85
STEAK WITH PEPPER SAUCE	2.50	2.25	1.95
(when available)			
SEA FOOD		2.50	2.25	1.95
ADOLPH'S SPECIAL LUNCHEON STEAK	3.25	2.95	2.75
SPENCER STEAK	3.75	3.50	3.25

LUNCHEON SALADS
CHICKEN SALAD	$1.40
TUNA SALAD	1.40
CHEF SALAD	1.65
CHEF SALAD half order	.90
COTTAGE CHEESE & FRUIT SALAD	1.40

WE CATER · FOOD TO GO
LUNCH HOUR LIMITED
We will gladly take your order by phone
BANQUET ROOM FOR UP TO 150 PERSONS

ENJOY A COCKTAIL WITH YOUR LUNCH

SANDWICHES
on sliced French Bread

Served with Salad or Cup of Soup or Vegetable or Spaghetti or Ravioli or French Fries

ROAST CROSS RIB OF BEEF	$1.50
HOT BEEF SANDWICH	1.70
HAM	1.50
GROUND CHUCK	1.50
with cheese	1.70
SKIRT STEAK	1.85
MEAT BALL	1.50
ITALIAN SAUSAGE	1.50
SALAMI & CHEESE	1.50
TURKEY (when available)	1.50
HOT TURKEY SANDWICH when available	1.70
CORNED BEEF (when available)	1.50

Sandwich with extra order of meat 25¢ extra
Sandwich on Bardoni French Bread 10¢ extra

PASTA
SPAGHETTI WITH MEAT SAUCE	1.00
RAVIOLI WITH MEAT SAUCE (when available)	1.50
HALF & HALF	1.25
RAVIOLI WITH MEAT BALLS (when available)	1.95
SPAGHETTI WITH MEAT BALLS	1.50
Served with Pasta and French Bread only	

LARGE SALAD	.50	SOUP BOWL	.75
SMALL SALAD	.35	SOUP CUP	.35
SMALL COTTAGE CHEESE & FRUIT BOWL			.50
FRENCH FRIES			.35
COKE or 7 Up	.25	SOFT DRINK PUNCH	.15
MILK	.20	COFFEE TEA OR SANKA	.15

EACH ITEM PER PERSON

PRICES DO NOT INCLUDE SALES TAX

Adolph's Luncheon menu. *Author's collection.*

Jeremy Nama started working as a busboy at Adolph's in 1986. He said, "Then I moved on to be a prep cook for banquets, then being 'on the line,' doing pastas at night. Then, they wanted me to help make the sauces in the mornings—starting at 6:30 a.m. I made the minestrone soup every day and clam chowder on Fridays in big sixty-quart pots—and, sometimes, we ran out of chowder!" He soon transitioned to sauté cook. Jeremy remembered, "After the earthquake, the city was a real mess. All the PG&E guys had voucher tickets and would come into Adolph's after 10:00 p.m., so we stayed open late to feed them." He worked there until late 1990. Jeremy is currently an arborist with Davey Tree Service in Santa Cruz.

Marla Novo is a second-generation native of Santa Cruz and went to Santa Cruz High School. Marla is currently the archivist at the Santa Cruz Museum of Art and History in Santa Cruz. Her father, Joe Novo, was a commercial fisherman and sold fish to all of the restaurants in Santa Cruz. Marla said, "I used to love going out to the Pontiac Grill with my friends after school. Their food and music were terrific—they had 1950s 'retro-style' décor with comfortable booths—the whole atmosphere was so much fun!" The Pontiac Grill was open from 1986 to 2002 and is a classic example of a "repurposed" building; the space had originally been a Pontiac car dealership, showroom and garage.

Linda Page and her family used to live just across the street from Rudy and Norma Camarlinghi on Sunnyside Avenue near Branciforte Avenue and Water Street. She recalls, "One afternoon, Norma asked if I wanted to come work for her at Adolph's, and that lasted for eighteen years." She said, "During a big banquet, which happened to be a non-smoking room, I saw a patron smoking, and I said, 'You give that to me' and I took it and just threw it outside. He was surprised, but I made my point." Everyone who has ever been a waiter or waitress has a "crazy story," and Linda shared hers. "One evening, I was serving a very hot dish or 'boat' of lasagna to a woman, and it somehow slid into her open purse! We comped her dinner, of course, but it was a real ruckus! I really made some wonderful friends there—still have them!"

Many restaurants had the MTV channel up on the television screens in their bars and lounges, hoping to attract a younger crowd. The pay-per-view music television channel MTV launched on August 1, 1981. Audiences could watch popular bands play (and interpret) their music twenty-four hours a day, seven days a week. Musicians, such as Blondie, Michael Jackson, Madonna, George Michael and Prince, performed their wildly popular songs and dances sometimes once an hour, and some even launched their latest albums on MTV.

Menu from La Manzana, Watsonville.
Courtesy of Leonard Santana.

Leonard Santana owns Manuel's in Aptos. His mother and father, Alice and Manuel Santana, owned and operated La Manzana on 100 West Lake Avenue in Watsonville during the early 1980s. The building and its huge courtyard were conceived by Manny and designed with the help of local landscape architect Roy Rydell. Leonard has a vast collection of the beautiful sketches, drawings and floor plans for La Manzana. The restaurant featured spectacular outdoor awnings, a stage that could comfortably seat twenty musicians, a delicatessen, a bakery, office spaces and a number of unique shops that were located downstairs and upstairs. As Leonard described, "The building inside and out was truly a work of art." Manny ordered all of the restaurant's meat from Ledyard's, the liquor from Young's, the beer from Favorite Brands and the fresh fish from Stagnaro's.

Marisa Schmidt was first hired as a hostess at Adolph's in 1983.

I had to make sure all the stations were ready before we opened, and went through the credit card slips and checks at closing; a lot of details involved. When I got to be a waitress, I had to learn about fish, sauces, different drinks and to remember these orders (especially the big tables) I drew everything on a paper placemat—we all called it "The Map!" We'd get so busy! But it was the most favorite job I ever had. In 1986, I started college at Long Beach State and would come home during the summer to make money. They always saved me a spot. The communication and preparation skills that I learned while waitressing transitioned to when I organized and prepared the food for our Surf Camps with my husband, Richard Schmidt.

Marisa and her husband operate The Richard Schmidt Surf School and their Costa Rica Surf & Yoga Retreats.

On a windy afternoon on the Santa Cruz Municipal Wharf, Dino Stagnaro sat at a table in his family's restaurant, Gilda's. He first started working there when he was thirteen years old.

That was forty-seven years ago....Soda crackers used to come packed in a cardboard box, and the busboys scooped them up with their bare hands into small bags to be served at the table with the homemade clam chowder. You couldn't do that now—there weren't food handler safety rules back then—so many rules now! But everything here is pretty much the same—the kitchen layout is the same, the menu is the same and our customer service is still always great.

The restaurant has been in the family since around 1930. Dino pointed out the beautiful wooden painted mural on the south side of the dining room. The mural depicts scenes of the wharf, fishermen at work, fishing boats and the old Casino. He said, "It used to be up in the restaurant Malio's, and when they closed, we had it moved here." Malio, Dino's brother and Malio J. Stagnaro's nephew, told the story of them bringing the heavy mural over to Gilda's. "The wood used for the painting is from an old barn up at UC and our construction guys hung it up. They had to do it in three pieces because our wall space in the dining area could only handle the main part. But we actually like the other two parts where they are." One hangs up in the waiting area and the other hangs up between the restrooms. Malio continued, "Over at my uncle's place, Malio's, it had originally faced the Monterey Bay, running in one long piece from one end of the bar to the other. We've never had to retouch it in any way. It's always been a real conversation piece!"

Dino described what it has been like dealing with purveyors over the years:

We used to order meat from Ledyard's and our linen came from Bartiteau's, and we ordered our wine through Joseph George, of course. In the old days, being a waiter was really an art form. Some worked here for years—all the prices and specials were memorized; everything was written down by hand. The math and the taxes were added up and all of this was done in their heads.

Dino said that they're looking forward to the upcoming Woodies on the Wharf in June, which has been held on the wharf since 1994. "It's one of the busiest weekends for us every year—well organized, always a great crowd."

Leo Stefani was the head chef at Adolph's in the 1980s. He described his memories of growing up in Santa Cruz and working at the many places described in this book, either tending bar or being the chef. He said, "Nonnie Bellandi (co-owner of Adolph's) had in his office a few picture frames hanging up on the wall. They were letters from purveyors thanking him

Chef Leo Stefani in the *Santa Cruz Sentinel* in 1984. *Author's collection.*

for always paying on time." Adolph's was one of the many places where Leo set up a brand-new washing machine for spin-drying lettuce for salads. "I had one made up at Facelli's, and that worked out great, so I just continued to do it!"

Adolph's Italian Family Style Restaurant was opened in 1940 on 69 Front Street, close to the wharf in Santa Cruz, by Adolfo and Georgia Camarlinghi. Their sons, Rudy and Bobby, went off to fight in World War II and returned home to help run the family business. Dee Weybright remembered, "It must have been in the early 1950s when we first went to eat at the old Adolph's on Front Street and then on to see the movie *Carousel* playing at the Del Mar. My husband, Art, worked downtown as the pharmacist at Melvin's Drugs." After the flood of 1955, Adolph's moved to 812 Front Street and then moved to 525 Water Street. Then came a substantial remodel of that building, and it officially reopened in 1959. Because of the close proximity to the Santa Cruz County Courthouse on Ocean Street, many lawyers, judges and other county employees regularly met there for lunch and then after work came back to enjoy the convivial atmosphere during "happy hour" in the Marlin Room Lounge. The Banquet Room was regularly used for meetings by the Elks, Masons, Lions, the Rotary Club, Chamber of Commerce and the Realtor Association.

In 1982, the family sold Adolph's to Nonnie and Polly Bellandi and Al Schlarman of San Jose. They kept the same menu and high standards of service, and the place continued to be a destination favorite. Many of the regular customers called ahead and requested the same booth every time. "Family Style" began with a huge bowl of homemade minestrone soup with baskets of French bread and croutons, then salad, then bowls of homemade pasta, then a choice of entrées and vegetables. Well known for its fantastic service, many patrons requested "so and so's section." Everyone in Santa Cruz remembers their delicious homemade raviolis. You could order them to-go by the dozen—frozen and packed in flat white boxes—or if you brought your own container, as many customers did, that was fine too. Sharon Nystrom Watson recalled, "We used to call ahead at

Adolph's and take in our own big saucepans for their raviolis and thick minestrone soup—really perfect for when company came to visit!" One morning, Nonnie made a wise business decision: he ordered televisions to be installed in the bar so that he could watch his beloved football dynasty of the 1980s: the San Francisco 49ers. Adolph's was sold for good in 2003, auctioning off most of its kitchen equipment and furniture.

Lori Evans was born in Santa Cruz and went to Santa Cruz High School. She began working at Adolph's when she was a teenager. She started making salads and setting up the popular Sunday buffet before she became a hostess and, finally, a waitress. She said, "You learn a lot of people skills, and it helps if you have a really good memory. It's a great part-time job for when you're young or as a second income helping support a family."

Jerri Tupper is Lori's sister, and she was also born in Santa Cruz and went to Santa Cruz High School. In the summer of 1968, Jerri said, "I began working at Adolph's, making all of their dinner salads. Then I took on the busy day shift as a waitress in the Marlin Room Lounge. My favorite thing to recommend to patrons was the skirt steak with mushrooms or the manicotti. Orders were all handwritten and put up on the carousel wheel. I had a lot of fun working there—made a lot of friends. It was such a great experience!"

Adolph's employees. Jerri Tupper is holding a plate of pasta. *Photograph by author.*

Jennifer Watson-Wolf was hired as a hostess at Adolph's in 1984. She said, "I sat guests, took care of credit cards, et cetera then worked the banquets then was hired as a waitress. Those years were the busiest times, and it was really like a big family. My fellow employees were so much fun to work with—we all covered each other's shifts and hung out after work." She learned a lot about work ethic and accommodating all kinds of tourists and regular patrons. During this time, smoking was still allowed in restaurants. Jenn said, "Waiting for a table to open up in the non-smoking section was often a forty-five-minute wait." Or they could choose to sit in the Marlin Room Lounge, a bit noisy and smoky with a vintage cigarette machine. Jenn also got used to taking drink orders. "If one customer ordered a regular martini and another had a martini but made with a pricier brand, the bartender would point this out by using a special coaster under that glass." Jenn said, "I looked forward to going to work every day!"

Gerry Turgeon owned the "trailblazing" Front Street Brewery from 1984 to 2001.

At the time, Front Street Brewery was only the fourth "brewpub" in California and was the sixth in the nation! I studied viticulture at UC Davis and was a home beer-brewer already. I designed all the pumps, filtration equipment and layout of tanks by myself. I didn't want to be in an industrial zone, and found the building on Front Street had potential since it was so close to the Pacific Garden Mall. We got a low-risk "Small Beer Manufacturer" license. The ordinance was that whatever hours you were open selling alcohol, the kitchen also had to be open. In sixteen years, I never got a violation. I sponsored adult soccer teams and everyone came in to watch their favorite teams. We got all of our produce from Watsonville Coast Produce. We did all the bottling by hand and sold to local liquor stores and markets. In the mid-1980s, I got an Apple II computer for doing spreadsheets and then a PC. Made it so much easier for handling accounts receivable and our inventory.

China Szechuan had a terrific location downtown, where the Downtowner used to be on Cathcart Street. Its co-owner was Richard Lee Sum, and it was in business from 1979 to 2007. The chef was Ming Chan Yuen—a famous name in Santa Cruz for years—who was instrumental in creating the fabulous Szechuan dishes at the New Riverside.

Above: 2525 advertisement in a Miss California Pageant program from 1980. *Author's collection.*

Left: Gerry Turgeon, owner of the Front Street Brewery. *Courtesy of Gerry Turgeon.*

Eli Bariteau, owner of Bariteau's Cleaners, was also a part-owner of the restaurant 2525, which was located in downtown Soquel, from 1979 to 1991. It was considerably upscale and exciting, and it had a terrific selection of wines. Leo Stefani helped to set up 2525's kitchen during its first few months of operation.

PART II
THE LOMA PRIETA EARTHQUAKE

At 5:04 p.m. on October 17, 1989, the Loma Prieta earthquake struck and lasted for approximately fifteen seconds—it measured 6.9 on the Richter scale. It rocked the entire Bay Area and was responsible for three deaths in Santa Cruz County (sixty-three in Northern California) and many injuries. It changed Santa Cruz County forever; many residences and buildings were marked uninhabitable. Hundreds of restaurant workers had to file for unemployment after the quake; claims had to be filed online via the computers at the Employment Development Department (EDD). People quickly found computers to be true lifelines.

Peggy Dolgenos of Cruzio Internet recalled, "After the earthquake, the entire Santa Cruz County area was without power and the telephone for some time. Business leaders began to realize, more than ever, that they needed

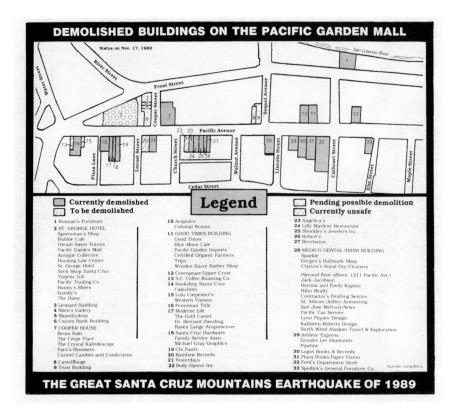

Map of Pacific Avenue earthquake damage in 1989. Each year, many people gather at the town clock in downtown Santa Cruz to observe the anniversary of the earthquake, which occurred on October 17, 1989, at 5:04 p.m. *Courtesy of graphic artist Michael Seal Riley, also known as Sizemo Graphics.*

to really communicate during the intense planning and reconstruction of the downtown area."

In the first days after the earthquake, India Joze was one of the few places that remained open and still served food in downtown Santa Cruz. Jozseph recalled, "I had all of my woks fired up; we just brought out tables and chairs, and everything was outside!" Gerry of the Front Street Brewery said, "My customers were all set to watch the 1989 World Series and the quake hit! My manager cleared out all of the food, and we donated it to 'ground zero' at the Civic Auditorium. The chain link fence was up for a while, closing off downtown, but we re-opened soon after, since our building was all right." Joe Hall also remembers the aftermath:

The Cooper House and the Santa Cruz Museum of Art and History. This picture was taken on October 20, 1989, from the corner of Front and Cooper Streets. The museum is the building behind the little white fence. *Photograph by author.*

First thing was to fence off the most affected area so that nobody else would get hurt and that nothing was stolen or looted. Pacific Avenue between Cathcart Street and the Town Clock was completely closed off. Under close supervision, there were a few shop owners who "maybe" were allowed to run in and retrieve their cash register or other valuables. I think after a couple of days, the wharf businesses reopened and did a bit better. There's a Quarterly Sales Report that shows the sales tax before and after the earthquake. For the downtown area—pre-earthquake in 1989—in the third quarter for eating and drinking places, sales were $536,500. The next quarter, sales were $328,800—a drop of 38.7 percent, showing an immediate impact.

The Chamber of Commerce and Cultural Council of Santa Cruz County and the Downtown Association came to be known as the "Phoenix Partnership." They worked on building huge four-thousand-square-foot tent pavilions for the downtown area, which helped many businesses make it through the holiday season. Ned Van Valkenberg said, "Our workers put up the tents in two days, and we even installed a floor in the Bookshop Santa Cruz tent."

A food pavilion for restaurants was also set up in the temporary downtown structures. Soon, a useful directory of open businesses was published and passed around with the title "We Survived!" and urged people to "shop local." One of these local businesses (a favorite eatery since 1948) was Zoccoli's Delicatessen. They continued to serve fresh sandwiches and homemade lasagna from their own ten-foot-by-thirty-foot trailer that had been set up in an empty lot on Cedar Street. After working in the trailer for eighteen months, Zoccoli's returned to Pacific Avenue. The tent pavilions stayed up until mid- to late 1992.

Highway 17 was completely closed by a massive landslide that was caused by the Loma Prieta earthquake; the closure lasted for over six long weeks. The landslide occurred between Granite Creek Road near Scotts Valley and Route 9 at Los Gatos, roughly an eleven-mile stretch. The closure affected, at the time, over twenty-three thousand commuters and delivery trucks daily. Some commuters just stayed over the hill in motels to be near their places of work. Many people drove an alternate route: Highway 1 going north, then over Highway 92 that connected to 280 going south to San Jose, which added an extra forty minutes each way. Ridesharing and carpooling was a godsend, as was the increased bus service. People cheered when Highway 17 reopened to through traffic on November 17, 1989.

The Loma Prieta earthquake affected the entire business community, including a wide circle of purveyors, whose own companies and services were interrupted. After they had built such strong personal connections over the years, they could only hope for the best for their customers. It was really tough to recover; they faced not being paid for products that had already been used or were no longer accessible. Purveyors wondered what would happen to their own unsold inventory and were anxious about the sudden disruption of their own work schedule. Insurance companies sent out inspectors, and the Federal Emergency Management Agency (FEMA) came to help out with emergency relief, but the long waiting period was stressful. Hardworking restaurant owners, and all business owners in general, struggled during the long months of reconstruction. The next few years were a time of readjustment.

POPULAR DRINKS OF THE 1980s

Between the Sheets: In a cocktail shaker filled with ice, pour one-half of an ounce of light Rum, one-half of an ounce of Cognac, one-half of an ounce of Triple Sec, one-half of an ounce of fresh lemon juice and one-half of an ounce of simple syrup; shake and strain into a Coupe glass; garnish with a lemon rind curl.

Harry MacElhone from Harry's New York Bar in Paris is credited for this recipe back in the 1920s. It's similar to a Sidecar but is made with equal parts Rum and Cognac. Ordering it out loud is somewhat provocative. The BTS made a big comeback in the 1980s as another drink featuring Rum.

Long Island Iced Tea: In a Highball glass full of ice, pour one-half of an ounce each of Rum, Vodka, Whiskey, Tequila and Gin, one-half of an ounce of Triple Sec and one-half of an ounce of fresh lemon juice; stir well, then top off with cola; garnish with a lemon wedge.

A Long Island Iced Tea is a refreshing drink that you can "nurse" for a good hour. A bartender, Bob "Rosebud" Butt at the Oak Beach Inn in Long Island, New York, invented this cocktail in 1972. It dares the person ordering it to see if it really does taste like iced tea

Matchbooks from Santa Cruz Hotel Bar & Grille, the Tea Cup and DeLaveaga Golf Lodge. *Cocktails prepared by author. Photograph by author. Author's collection.*

(it does). The coloring is similar to real iced tea, and the added fresh lemon juice and lemon wedge help to complete the look. Daring, because of a possible hangover due to mixing of spirits, and pricey.

Tequila Sunrise: In a Highball glass full of ice, pour two ounces of Tequila, three ounces of fresh orange juice, do not stir: carefully float one ounce of Grenadine syrup on top; garnish with an orange peel.

This cocktail was created by Bobby Lozoff and Billy Rice in the early 1970s at the Trident Restaurant and Bar in Sausalito, California. It still is a go-to cocktail when ordering Tequila (people often order an extra shot of Tequila on the side) and is a very pretty drink. "Tequila Sunrise" was a popular song written by the Eagles in 1973. Also popular is the Tequila Sunset; simply substitute the Grenadine syrup with Blackberry syrup.

Chapter 6

The Purveyors

These are the stories of the people behind the scenes, who are in the business of serving the restaurants—the purveyors who keep the restaurants humming. These are the people who supply the tablecloths and linen, wine and liquor, bread and rolls, equipment like pots and pans, computers, meat and seafood, fresh produce, ice and the company that regularly cleans the grease traps. Their perspective is important, because they are also members of the restaurant community and personally know the impacts that were made over this fifty-year period.

Getting in and out of Santa Cruz is a challenge; motorists traveling from San Jose over Highway 17 have to learn to prepare for its winding roads and the unfortunate traffic jams. The four-lane highway is over 26.5 miles going one way and 26.5 miles coming back, with sharp turns, blind curves and, during the summer months, heavy traffic. Delivery trucks carrying loads of wine, meat and seafood, produce and bread face these same road conditions as tourists but know from experience that to work around the crowd of cars, it's wise to schedule their routes to leave early in the morning and return early in the afternoon.

John Bargetto and his family own the Bargetto Family Winery and Tasting Room in Soquel, which recently celebrated its eighty-fifth anniversary. He said:

I started working for the family business when I was in the fourth grade, digging ditches and helping out wherever needed. One of my earliest memories of work during my high school years were the afternoons. My job was to drive

a big truck delivering boxes of wine bottles to the restaurants, but first, I had
to hand over the invoices, which had to be paid before I unloaded their boxes!

The 1955 and 1982 floods were both huge challenges for their business, and of course, so was the 1989 earthquake. John saw the Soquel community come together and help each other out. He has made many wonderful personal connections with his loyal customers, including all of the big restaurants in the area such as the Shadowbrook, Casablanca, Stagnaro's and Adolph's to name just a few. John said, "The computer has helped in lots of ways with managing our inventory and accounts."

Barry Bariteau is a third-generation native of Santa Cruz and managed his family's business, Bariteau's Cleaners, which had served locals since 1908. His dad, Eli, was a member of a group of local businessmen called the Dirty Dozen; this group regularly met for lunch and played dice using leather cylinder cups. Eli was a regular at Adolph's, which was located just across the way on Water Street. Bariteau's supplied all of the major restaurants and hotels throughout the county with linens, aprons, towels, napkins, tablecloths and floor mats. Barry said, "Everything got especially busy during the holidays with company parties and banquets, and also during the wedding season, when people came in with their special orders." Bariteau's had a drive-up window and provided dry cleaning services to the police, fire and sheriff's departments for all of their uniforms. As a child, Barry remembers that his whole family enjoyed going out to dinner at the Santa Cruz Hotel. Barry comes from a family of athletes and loves to play golf. He also played on the varsity baseball team with his friend Steve Pollock (the author's husband) at Harbor High School in the early 1980s.

Barry's memory of the 1989 earthquake is still crystal clear:

The whole town was without power for a long time, so every night, I had to
drive a big company truck over the mountain roads to our plant in San Jose,
since Highway 17 was damaged and closed for a while. All of the hotels
really depended on us; the workers coming in to help with the bridges and
roads depended on us. It was a really crazy, intense time.

Bariteau's Cleaners finally closed its doors in December 2018.

Peggy Dolgenos and Chris Neklason are the co-owners of Cruzio Internet, which was instrumental in providing local restaurants in Santa Cruz County with email account and computer help during the 1980s. In 1993, the Internet really changed the advertising world, and restaurants had to respond. In addition to placing old-fashioned ads in the local newspaper

Premium Wines from Bargetto Winery

Effective April 1, 1977

White Wines	10ths	5ths
Chablis	1.35	2.49
Chardonnay	1.85	3.50
Chenin Blanc	1.50	2.75
Moscato Amabile	1.75	2.95
Chaucer's Mead	1.75	2.95
Johannisberg Riesling		4.00

Rosé Wines

	10ths	5ths
Vin Rosé Dolce	1.35	2.49
Zinfandel Rosé		2.75

Red Wines

	10ths	5ths
Burgundy	1.35	2.49
Grenache		2.75
Zinfandel 1975		2.95
Barbera		3.50
Ruby Cabernet		2.95

Santa Cruz Cellars Dinner Wines
A semi-premium wine for everyday drinking

	Gal.	½ Gal.	5ths
Chablis	5.89	3.49	1.89
Rhine Wine	5.89	3.49	1.89
Vin Rosé	5.89	3.49	1.89
Burgundy	5.89	3.49	1.89
Zinfandel	5.89	3.49	1.89
Ruby Cabernet	5.89	3.49	1.89

Special Dessert Wines
Selected by Bargetto Winery

Beccaro Marsala Wines	23 ounce decanters
Almond Marsala	4.59
Orange Marsala (Mandarino)	4.59
Coffee Marsala	4.59
Strawberry Marsala (Fragola)	4.59
Walnut Marsala	4.59
Cherry Marsala	4.59
Moka Cream (Opale Decanter)	7.69
Moka Cream (Marakas Decanter)	6.19
Dry Marsala Wine	3.97
Apricots in Marsala Wine	5.75
Cherries in Marsala Wine	5.75

Fruit Wines	10ths	5ths
Plum Wine	1.35	2.49
Apricot Wine	1.35	2.49
Pear Wine	1.35	2.49
Peach Wine	1.35	2.49
Strawberry Wine	1.35	2.49
Raspberry Wine	1.85	3.49
Olallieberry Wine	1.85	3.49
Honey Wine	1.35	2.49
Brambleberry Wine	1.85	3.49
Blackberry Wine	1.85	3.49

Aperitif Wines	Gals.	½-Gals.	5ths
Dry Vermouth	5.89	3.49	1.49
Sweet Vermouth	5.89	3.49	1.49

Rare Dessert Wines

	5ths
Moscato D'Oro 1951	14.95
Moscato D'Oro 1946	35.00

Sparkling Wines

	Mags.	5ths	10ths	Splits
Champagne	5.98	2.99	1.70	.99
Pink Champagne	5.98	2.99	1.70	.99
Sparkling Burgundy	5.98	2.99	1.70	.99
Cold Duck	5.98	2.99	1.70	.99

Chef Luigi Red Wine Vinegar
Aged Two Years in Wood

Gals.	4.99
½ Gals.	2.99
5ths	1.49
10ths	.89

(10% discount on case lots.
Does not assort with wine for discount.)

10% Case Discount on all orders
of one or more cases.

Case Quantities

Gals.	4 per case
½ Gals.	6 per case
5ths	12 per case
23 oz. decanters	12 per case
10ths	24 per case

Bargetto's menu from 1977, Soquel. On the verso side of this menu is a brief history of the winery and an order form listing shipping charges. *Author's collection.*

113

Bariteau's Linen Service sign. *Photograph by author. Courtesy of Barry Bariteau.*

and a listing in the telephone book, restaurant owners decided that it was a good marketing idea to get a computer. Cruzio was there to work with restaurant owners on this new venture. In 2019, Cruzio celebrated its thirtieth anniversary as a local business.

John Flocchini is a member of the family that owns the Durham Meat Company. He said:

> *I remember, very fondly, eating at Adolph's many times as a kid with my family. We loved that place! Besides sneaking down to Santa Cruz* [from Los Gatos] *with my friends to surf as often as I could, we had a summer place in Bonny Doon where our families spent lots of time. In fact, we just celebrated a family get-together in Aptos last fall, and we visited the Santa Cruz Beach Boardwalk, where my eighty-six-year-old father joined us in riding the Giant Dipper. The area holds a lot of great memories for our family.*

John runs the fifty-five-thousand-acre Durham Bison Ranch near Wright, Wyoming. Rich Flocchini is John's uncle, and he said:

> *Our Durham Meat Company offices and cold storage plant were located in downtown San Jose, where the Shark Tank is now.* [The nickname

114

comes from it being the home of the San Jose Sharks, a National Hockey League team. It is an indoor sports arena currently known as the SAP Center at San Jose.] *The city's redevelopment agency decided that's what was going to be built there, so we moved everything to Reno, Nevada, where we already had a good base, including our longtime customer U.S. Foods in Sacramento. Del Monte Meats took over our San Jose and Santa Cruz accounts.*

Rich remembers the years he spent selling his family's premium meats to restaurants in Santa Cruz, including the Santa Cruz Hotel and Adolph's.

Santa Cruz has a special meaning for our family, because we used to own property in Bonny Doon, had eleven acres, lots of horses. One winter, a big storm blew a tree down, made a huge hole, and so our dad went to Davenport and arranged for a truckload of cement to be delivered, and he made us a gigantic pool. It was fifty feet long, thirty feet wide and twelve feet deep, with a giant stainless-steel slide—it was a lot of fun! The old house had a long, covered porch and, of course, a big barbeque area with picnic tables. We used to ride our horses to the old tavern, The Lost Weekend.

Rich now runs Sierra Meat and Seafood located in Reno, Nevada.

Bert George is the third generation to work in his family's business, Joseph George Distributors, which started out in Santa Cruz in 1940. He remembered, "Our warehouse was on Seventeenth Avenue and Ledyard [because it had to be near the train track spur], and we delivered beer and wine to restaurants all over Santa Cruz County. It was standard practice for our Santa Cruz drivers to keep a close watch on the wave action, and they kept their surfboards in their trucks, ready to go!" Before the 1970s, people had simply a choice of either red or white wine or they ordered a cocktail in the restaurant. Bert said, "But then, wine really came on strong, and the wait staff began suggesting wines to pair with specials. The classic phrase, 'I'll just have a glass of Chardonnay,' well, that's when the industry really took off!" Bert and his family run their retail wine shop, Joseph George Fine Wines, in the Willow Glen area of San Jose.

In 2016, Joseph George Fine Wines collaborated with the NHS, Inc. Skateboard Company based in Santa Cruz, along with the Santa Cruz Museum of Art and History, to celebrate the thirtieth anniversary of the *Screaming Hand* design of the artist Jim Phillips. Joseph George Fine Wines produced the 3.0-litre double magnum bottle of cabernet

Above: Durham Meat Co. trucks parked in front of their San Jose location. *Courtesy of Rich Flocchini.*

Opposite, inset: The artist Jim Phillips signed this 3.0-litre double magnum bottle of cabernet sauvignon, which was made by the Martin Ranch winery in the Santa Cruz Mountains to commemorate the thirtieth year of his *Screaming Hand* design. *Photograph by author. Courtesy of Joseph George Fine Wines.*

sauvignon made by the Martin Ranch Winery in the Santa Cruz Mountains as a commemoration. Since 1985, the *Screaming Hand* has been the main logo for NHS, Inc. The president of NHS, Inc., Bob Denike, as well as Richard Novak, the owner of NHS, Inc., and the artist Jim Phillips all signed—etched—the bottle. In addition, Joseph George Fine Wines produced a limited quantity of thirty standard-size 750 ml wine bottles that were also specially signed—etched—Jim Phillips.

Taylor Fontana's dad, Richard Fontana, owned Ledyard's Supply Co., which sold restaurant supplies, including stoves, pans, slicers, paper goods, crockery and glassware. In 1978, Aldo H. Fontana and his son, Richard, bought Ledyard's from H.H. Ledyard. Both Aldo and Richard emphasized true customer service. Taylor said, "Their main philosophy was to keep the customer happy, and they were available at all times during the day or night. They suffered from a huge loss of product during the 1989 earthquake, but they moved what they could onto tractor trailers, and they ran the business from there." The big-name competitors may have offered slightly lower prices, but Ledyard's knew the needs of the local restaurants. Taylor said his dad was quick to install computers and set up email accounts. When describing his dad, Taylor said, "He really liked being open minded to different systems for the future of the company. When my dad finally sold the business and retired in 2011, he received a hefty buyout, and he divided all of it up among his longtime employees." Taylor and his brother, Ryan, own Malone's Grille in Scotts Valley. Years ago, the building was a tavern called the Rusty Lantern.

For many years, Taylor's grandfather Aldo H. Fontana served as the president of Parisian Bakeries, Inc. in San Francisco. In 1969, Aldo bought the Modern Baking Company, a six-thousand-square-foot building on Cedar Street in Santa Cruz. The bakery had been in business since 1934 and had been owned by the Sandas family since 1946. In the 1960s, the company's print advertisements featured a character called Toulouse Bordeaux, who was drawn in the likeness of the painter Toulouse-Lautrec, and asked, "The Modern Baking Company's resident artist loves Matzo Balls and Bordeaux French Bread. How about you?"

The H. H. Ledyard company, long known as a supply depot for grocery firms, is changing, as the equipment in this photo indicates, to specialize in hotels and restaurants. Because of the steady upsurge of the larger grocery chains and the gradual demise of the small grocery stores, the gradually switchover is taking place. At left, showing how large restaurant pans can get, is Walter Naef, restaurant and supply manager, and at right with a pizza paddle is David Ledyard, company president.

Ledyard's Restaurant Supply—specializing in hotels and restaurants. Walter Naef and David J. Ledyard on January 26, 1969. *Courtesy of the* Santa Cruz Sentinel.

Their fleet of trucks distributed to all the major restaurants in Santa Cruz County, and it had a contract to provide all of the rolls and breads for the Fort Ord Military Base in Salinas, near the Monterey Bay. Parisian Bakeries, Inc. closed its doors forever on August 19, 2005, after producing San Francisco's signature sourdough bread for over 149 years, along with the other bread companies, Colombo and Toscana Breads.

Paulino Reyes is the owner of Paulino's Bakery in Watsonville. He began baking forty years ago and has been delivering his delicious fresh breads and rolls to restaurants in Santa Cruz County for over eighteen years, assuming many of the delivery routes from the old Parisian Bakeries, Inc. His customers include the Stagnaro Bros. Seafood, Inc., Splash! and other restaurants on the Santa Cruz Municipal Wharf. Paulino's bread is also featured at the AT&T Pebble Beach Pro-Am Golf Tournament and many restaurants in the city of Monterey. Paulino has two huge Baxter Rotating Rack Ovens and uses the giant stacks of three thousand bread pans that he purchased from the old Colombo Bakery. He said he starts working at 5:00 a.m. with seven employees and three delivery trucks. Summertime is always busy; he said, "I talk with my customers every day—'What do you need?'"

Sara Brown and her husband, Darrel, have owned Pete's Outflow Technicians since 1971, and they service the grease traps in restaurants and hotels throughout Santa Cruz County. When they bought the business from Pete Walquist (owner since 1953), they only had one truck, and today, they have four trucks. Adolph's was a regular customer for years, and their current longtime customers include Manuel's and other accounts all along the Esplanade in Capitola. Sara said, "There's been a lot of changes over the years. For instance, what used to be county regulations are now state regulations, plus we have to be up-to-date on California's strict vehicle air quality requirements." The 1989 earthquake affected their business because "some of the restaurants we serviced were closed for months during reconstruction, and some are gone forever." They've stayed fairly small, enjoying the friendships they've made over the years. Sara and Darrel's sons, grandsons and nephew help to run the business.

Jim Beauregard and his family have owned Shopper's Corner in the Eastside Santa Cruz neighborhood since 1938. They feature an extensive selection of wines, fresh local produce and a full-service butcher shop. When the 1989 earthquake hit, Jim was at home, and he said, "Right away, I went to the store—the employees got together, swept up all the broken glass and debris and my dad arranged for several pickup trucks to drive it all to the dump. The next day, we were open at 8:00 a.m.!" Their classic neon clock face and sign that say "Time to Shop" is a landmark in Eastside Santa Cruz. Jim's son, Ryan, runs Beauregard Vineyards in Bonny Doon, which used to be known as The Lost Weekend.

John Tara works in his office inside the Stagnaro Bros. Seafood, Inc. warehouse on Washington Street in downtown Santa Cruz, which has been their business location since 1947. John said, "I started working here while still in high school with my grandfather and my father." They currently have six trucks and thirteen employees. "We make all of our ice ourselves, right here." They deliver north up to Pescadero, and all the way

Shopper's Corner. Their classic neon sign and clock are landmarks in the Eastside neighborhood of Santa Cruz. *Photograph by author. Courtesy of Jim Beauregard.*

south to San Juan Bautista and Carmel, but they mostly maintain a regular busy schedule delivering to local restaurants. They also operate their retail store, Stagnaro Bros. Outdoor Fish Market. It is the largest outdoor fish market on the West Coast and has been in operation since 1937. Sightseers regularly walk by to look at the freshly caught fish; perhaps they have never seen such large, whole, fresh salmon up close. John said, "It's all a part of the wharf experience!"

In addition, there is the Stagnaro Bros. Restaurant, which is located at the outer end of the wharf. All three locations recycle every bit of cardboard. John said that, immediately after the 1989 earthquake, they were fortunate and managed to borrow a giant generator that kept their freezers going at the warehouse. In 2017, the Stagnaro Bros. Restaurant celebrated its eightieth year in business and offered a special menu that featured 1937 prices. Their motto is "Caught today, cooked today, your home or ours. Buon Appetito!"

Jeanne Whiting's dad, Ray Piexoto, worked the the Union Ice Company in Santa Cruz for forty-one years, the last eighteen as the general manager, and retired in 1982. The Union Ice Company helped

Stagnaro Bros. Seafood, Inc. is the largest outdoor fish market on the West Coast and has been operating since 1937. *Photograph by author. Courtesy of John Tara.*

play a significant part in feeding the armed forces during World War II. After the local crops of apricots, beans, Brussels sprouts and other fruits and vegetables were harvested, they were taken by trucks to the Santa Cruz Fruit Packing Company on Bronson Street in the Seabright neighborhood. After being trimmed and picked over, the fruits and vegetables were taken over to the Union Ice Company's plant on Laurel Street and Chestnut Avenue to be fast-frozen. The Union Ice Company was an important employer in Santa Cruz, with three eight-hour shifts every twenty-four hours. The company also sold ice to the Boardwalk as well as offering cold storage for future sales of fruits and vegetables. Jeanne remembers, "My dad always planned months ahead for having enough corn on the cob ready for July Fourth, always a favorite at the Boardwalk!" For years, many restaurants regularly had their ice delivered by the Union Ice Company trucks, and Ted Burke of the Shadowbrook remembers them very well. In August 1990, the old Union Ice Company building was completely destroyed in a terrible fire.

Gary Manfre owns Watsonville Coast Produce. He said, "I started out in 1974 with one flatbed truck, three bobtail trucks and ten employees." Today, he has thirty trucks and one hundred employees. He is proud to deliver

Above: An ice pick that was given away to customers of the Union Ice Company, Santa Cruz. *Author's collection.*

Left: Watsonville Coast Produce. This photograph of an early 1930s handtruck was taken in Gary Manfre's office hallway. *Photograph by author.*

fresh, local produce to all of the big restaurants in Santa Cruz, including the Shadowbrook. He believes in always making a personal connection with his customers. Gary said, "We recycle virtually everything, including cardboard, office paper, plastic wrap, nylon pallet straps, Styrofoam boxes, plastic and cardboard corner boards, wood waste, motor oil, coolants and scrap metal. Our recycling efforts have resulted in a 75 percent reduction in what we send to the landfill." He said, "We're so fortunate to live where you can find fresh vegetables and fresh fruit all year round!" His business has survived freezes, the drought years, floods and storms. When the big earthquake happened in 1989, Gary said, "We donated all that we could—we just gave it all away to whoever needed the food." He recalled that his parents used to take the family to Castagnola's and Facelli's "for really special occasions."

Chapter 7

1990s and Beyond

A fter the earthquake, part of the strategic plan that helped to bring the tourists back to Santa Cruz included creating television spots, radio promotions and print ads. Local hotels offered package deals for golfers and fishermen, and some provided maps of the Santa Cruz Mountain wineries. Restaurant owners spent more of their marketing budgets on developing websites and reaching out to potential customers. UCSC's enrollment numbers stayed somewhat level, showing only minimum growth for the decade. Beginning in the fall of 1990 there were 9,234 students enrolled, and ending in June 1999, that number had increased to just 10,606 (including the graduate students). The Census recorded that the population in Santa Cruz County in 1990 was 229,734, showing a steady growth, in spite of the earthquake, road repairs and construction sites everywhere.

DJ Marc Peterson recalled his time as the manager of Mike's Soul Food. The restaurant was located on the corner of River and Water Streets (previously the site of Manoff's Rancho Burger) and was in business from 2001 to 2003. It was one of the very few African American–owned restaurants in Santa Cruz County. DJ Marc said, "We kept the old wagon wheel motif décor, because you could say it added to the unique atmosphere! We only cooked with fresh and local produce, which we ordered from Watsonville Coast Produce. Collard greens, onions and yams—everything was organic and fresh." He continued:

> Because of California State regulations, we couldn't use bacon grease, but instead, we used a very light oil for frying. The catfish was outstanding,

it was a big seller, just like our fried chicken. Everyone raved about our cornbread and our barbecued ribs. Mike Mitchell, the owner, put in an application for a liquor license but, unfortunately, had back issues, so we had to close for him to deal with that. But it was a good experience, and I enjoyed myself.

Jenn Watson-Wolf and her husband, Horst Wolf, owned the popular Santa Cruz Sandwiches from 2004 to 2012. The restaurant was located directly across from Harbor High School, and Jenn recalls, "Parents would come in and set up monthly accounts for their kids, and there was always a steady group of medical personnel from the nearby Dominican Hospital calling in their pickup orders."

Leonard Santana of Manuel's said, "There are no big-screen televisions in my restaurants, because I really love it when people enjoy our food and actually talk with each other!" The Santana family also owns a popular restaurant in San Juan Bautista called Jardines de San Juan. In 2015, Manuel's celebrated its fiftieth year in business.

Bill Prime understands the restaurant industry from the ground up; he first worked as a dishwasher, bussed tables, was a banquet waiter, a line chef and then became a manager. Bill was the chef at Zelda's in Capitola for many years and was the executive chef at the Compass Grille and Bar in the Dream Inn from 1991 to 1999. Bill and his team won the Santa Cruz Clam Chowder Cook Off, which has been held on the Santa Cruz Municipal Wharf many times. He said, "There was a contest for dreaming up the new name of the restaurant after the Compass. I came up with the name—Mainsail!" Bill is currently the executive director of dining services at UCSC. There are approximately ten thousand UCSC students enrolled on the meal plan, which serves three meals a day in five dining halls. Every day, Bill balances the menus to reflect the food choices and preferences of the students, and he takes food allergies and various dietary restrictions into consideration. Bill buys fresh vegetables and fruit from local resources. He also collects vintage restaurant menus and has some terrific stories.

A review of the trends and impacts of Santa Cruz restaurants for the past five decades: During World War II and the 1940s, rationing forced people to make do with less; it also made the people of Santa Cruz feel grateful for their access to local crops and fresh fish. "Car Culture" in the 1950s inspired savvy restaurant owners to discover that their largest dining rooms were their own parking lots. Businesses prospered in the 1960s, partly because customers chose to pay their bills with their new credit cards. The 1970s brought an awareness of "natural" and fresh ingredients, as chefs chose to move away from processed foods. In the 1980s, computers helped restaurant owners schedule staff, pay bills and manage perishable inventory. In the months after the 1989 Loma Prieta earthquake, there was tremendous community support; many of the businesses and restaurants survived because the people of Santa Cruz showed their loyalty by continuing to "shop locally" during reconstruction.

The greatest opportunity for the restaurant industry continues to be the trend of offering customers an "experience" with an accompanying storyline. For example, years ago, a building that used to be a cannery was converted into a popular restaurant. This historic research is utilized in all of its marketing—on the menus, posters and website. Another trend is incorporating a family tradition; for instance, special recipes are prepared in the exact same way that the owner's grandmother used to make them. Customers enjoy these historic connections and remember their significance, as well as the restaurant's great food and service.

Retro cuisines and décor fit in very well in a coastal tourist town; whether its a 1950s diner or a restaurant with a South Sea island atmosphere, visitors will be drawn to it. Bartenders can learn a lot by looking through vintage bartending manuals for cocktail recipes to add to their repertoire—perhaps

Tea Cup Restaurant in 1989. *Courtesy of Steve Hosmer, Stokes Signs.*

giving it a new or personal twist. Patrons enjoy learning the history of a drink and all of its variations.

Many of the people who were interviewed for this book said that their very first job was working at a restaurant. Whether they stayed in the restaurant business or went on to other kinds of work, they happily shared their stories and the memories they made there. The memory of dining out is a perfect example of how Santa Cruz County chooses to honor its roots.

Epilogue

The common thread in these oral histories of restaurant workers is that each person managed to find, deep within, their own initiative, self-determination and optimism. Despite man-made disasters (for instance, World War II) and natural disasters (the floods and the earthquake), these men and women showed up to work, knowing that they had to be prepared and ready for a hungry and thirsty crowd.

While conducting the interviews for this book, I heard many wonderful stories of ingenuity, can-do attitudes and, upon reflection after so many years, feelings of real accomplishment. Several of the women chefs and restaurant owners stand out; for example, the enterprising Cindy Lepore-Hart, Catherine Faris, Marcia McDougal and Suzanne Grelson Rom. I was thrilled to hear the old-fashioned, elbow-grease story of Cindy Lepore-Hart. "I set up and designed the new kitchen for Seychelle's all by myself, and laid the black and white tile floor by myself." I was impressed with Catherine Faris's creative approach when, at first, her business was short on capital. "I did a lot of research on limited partnership and drew up 'shares' so that people could then trade in for dinners at Primitzia." I admired the way Marcia McDougal managed so many enterprises at the same time—she ran the New Davenport Cash Store's bed-and-breakfast, baked and cooked for the restaurant and ran the Big Creek Pottery residential school; and through it all, she demonstrated her skill for organization. I enjoyed how Suzanne Grelson Rom described the sense of fun and good humor at her restaurant. Patrons returned for the special ambiance at L'Oustalou and raved about her delicious food.

Looking back at the history of these lost restaurants of Santa Cruz County, it is clear that there is a real depth of multicultural traditions. Before food trends, there were recipes passed down through generations of family cooks. Before online blogs, there were word-of-mouth recommendations and the restaurant reviews in the local newspapers. Those of us who live in Santa Cruz are fortunate to be so close to the Pacific Ocean and have such a rich agricultural heritage. Santa Cruz County continues to attract entrepreneurial chefs and inspire creativity.

Appendix

Restaurants

Acapulco
1116 Pacific Avenue
Santa Cruz
John Gularte
1967–2012
Mexican Cuisine

**Adolph's Italian Family Style
  Restaurant**
525 Water Street
Santa Cruz
Adolfo, Georgia, Rudy and Bobby
  Camarlinghi;
Nonnie and Polly Bellandi and Al
  Schlarman
1939–2003
Italian Cuisine

Albatross
2380 Portola Drive
Santa Cruz
1978–1986

Al Dente Ristorante
415 Seabright Avenue
Santa Cruz
Lucio Fanni
1980s
Italian Cuisine

Am-Pol
3601 Portola Drive
Santa Cruz
Ludwik and Vera Chrobok
Featuring a strolling violinist, Bart
  Cichocki
1969–1984
Polish Cuisine

Aoi Japanese Restaurant
4727 Scotts Valley Drive
Scotts Valley
David Kimura
1978–1990
Japanese Cuisine

The Ark
112 Capitola Avenue
Santa Cruz
Greta and Ethan Hamm
1980–1984

Avenue Grille
275 Pacific Avenue and then
   698 Pacific Avenue
Santa Cruz
H.A. Karras
1940s–1950s

The Bandstand
201 Esplanade Street
Capitola
Babe Yakobovich
1946–1975

Bayview Hotel
8041 Soquel Drive
Aptos
Fred Toney; Bill and Vera Guzules
1878, hotel; various restaurants,
   various owners

Bea's Koffee Kup
1209 Soquel Avenue
Santa Cruz
Bernice Burns
1977–2002

Benias
112 Capitola Avenue
Capitola
John and Vivian Benias
1951–1971
Owners were originally from
   Greece

Biwa
2623 Forty-First Avenue
Capitola
Donald Y. and Haruko Tanzawa
1969–1979
Japanese Cuisine

**Blacksmith Shop Char-
   Broiler**
3005 North Porter Street
Soquel
Loren D. Schobel and Donald D.
   Barton
1967–1976

Bosley's Drive-In
404 Water Street at Ocean Street
Santa Cruz
Jack Bosley
1946–1950

Broken Egg Omelet House
605 Front Street
Santa Cruz
There was another location on
   7887 Soquel Drive, Aptos
Barry L. Hutchison
1970–1998

Brookdale Lodge
11570 Highway 9
Brookdale
Judge James Harvey Logan; Dr.
   F.K. Camp; Barney Morrow;
   various owners
Opened in 1922 (with a few gap
   years); renovated in 2018

Bubble Bakery and Cafe
1530 Pacific Avenue
Santa Cruz
William and Leo Caiocca, Joe
    Costella and Felix Stiener
1946–1989 (destroyed in
    earthquake)

Carniglia's
49-A Santa Cruz Municipal Wharf
Santa Cruz
Mary P. and Marco Carniglia
1941–1979
Italian Cuisine

Carroll's Drive-In
615 Highway 1
Watsonville
Carroll Elwood
1950s

Casablanca
101 Main Street
Santa Cruz
Ray and Glyndean Luttrell
1951–1990s

Casa del Rey Hotel
Beach Street
Santa Cruz
Charles Canfield, Santa Cruz
    Seaside Company
1928–1989 (destroyed in
    earthquake)

Castagnola's
119 South River Street
Santa Cruz
Al and Bob Castagnola
1969–1979

Castle Dining Room
Also known as Scholl-Mar Castle,
    Casa del Mar, The Castle
1320 East Cliff Drive
Santa Cruz
Ivan Netoff and Fred Russell
1940s–1967

The Catalyst
821 Front Street and 1011 Pacific
    Avenue
Santa Cruz
Randall Kane; Joel Nelson
Opened in 1967; still open

Cathay Cafe
617 Pacific Avenue
Santa Cruz
Shoon and Sue Lim
1967–1997
Cantonese Cuisine

Cavalier Restaurant
127 Pacific Avenue, opposite
    Municipal Pier
Santa Cruz
Lucy E. and Charles S. Toshikian
Opened in 1949
Specialty was shish kebab

Cedar Street Cafe
411 Cedar Street
Santa Cruz
Mary Helen Chapell, Gwen
    Shupe, Tom O'Leary; Rita
    Calvert
1970s–1980s

Chachie's Hot Dogs
Santa Cruz Beach Boardwalk
  Concessionaire
400 Beach Street
Santa Cruz
Ottaviano Chachie
1980s

The Charles Dickens
9051 Soquel Drive
Aptos
Nancy J. Genge; Mary Eileen
  Petersen; Leon, Karin and Mary
  Fidrych
1974–1983

Chef Tong's
1601 Forty-First Avenue
Capitola
Francis Tong
1978–1985
Chinese Szechuan Cuisine

Chez Renee
9051 Soquel Drive
Aptos
John B. and Renee B. Chyle
1983–2000
French Cuisine

Chicken Villa
401 Front Street
Santa Cruz
Various owners
1944–1953

China Cafe
270 Soquel Avenue
Santa Cruz
Deck Soo Hoo
1964–1991
Chinese Cuisine

China Szechuan
221 Cathcart Street
Santa Cruz
Chef Ming Chan Yuen
1979–2007
Szechuan Cuisine

Chop Stick
437 Main Street
Watsonville
1970s
Chinese Cuisine

Circle Coffee Grill
Concrete Bridge
Capitola
Pete and Helen Pantages
1950s

Coast Creamery Fountain
359 Pacific Avenue
Santa Cruz
Lester and Lois Cuneo
1950s

College Daze Fountain
339 Pacific Avenue, and then 818
  Pacific Avenue
Harry Papalian
1937–1946

Colonial Inn
1602 Ocean Street
Santa Cruz
Don Stefani and Albert M. Pardini
1950–1968

The Cook Book Restaurant
207 Searidge Road
Aptos
Lionel and Alberta Barrigan
1968–1980

The Cooper House
110 Cooper Street
Santa Cruz
Max Walden; many restaurants,
  various owners
1971–1989 (destroyed in
  earthquake)

Costella's Chalet
6275 Highway 9
Felton
Lou, Bob and Edward Costella
1941–1984

Courtyard
2591 Main Street
Soquel
Frank A. Capriotti Jr.; Tom King
1971–1983

Cross Roads Bar-B-Q Drive-In
226 Washington Street
Santa Cruz
Leonard and Louise Klempnauer
1947–1960

Dang Me's
2605 Main Street
Soquel
1960s
Creekside Dining

Danny's Diner
2501 Soquel Drive
Santa Cruz
Mark Carmalinghi
1986–1995

Deer Park Tavern
Highway 1, Rio del Mar exit
Aptos
Nick J. (Shorty) Butriza
1933–1975

DeLaveaga Golf Lodge
401 Upper Park Road
Santa Cruz
John Bei and George Vomvolakis
1969–2016

Delmarette Fountain
1126 Pacific Avenue
Santa Cruz
Phyllis Ratzman
1937–1989

Del Monte Cafe
300 Walnut Street
Watsonville
Vince, Lucy and Pete Kovacich
1960s–1990s

The Depot
123 Washington Street
Santa Cruz
Larry Bourriague, Jerry Neilsen
  and Warren Penniman
1973–1975

Dick's
1116 Pacific Avenue
Santa Cruz
Dick H. Stampolis
1955–1962

Dietrich's (in the Holiday Inn)
611 Ocean Street
Santa Cruz
Dietrich Pahnke
1960s–1985

**Donato's Ristorante
  Napoletana**
Donato's Grotto
303 Beach Street
Santa Cruz
Richard J. Scotti
1974–1980

Donut Den
260 East Lake Avenue
Watsonville
Charles Delbovo
1950s

Downtowner
221 Cathcart Street
Santa Cruz
Howard C. and Mildred P. Lowe
1973–1979

Dutch Doll Pancake House
303 Beach Street
Santa Cruz
C. and S. Darquennes–Van Ael
1950s

The Edgewater
215 Esplanade
Capitola
Louis J. and Arline L. Aluffi, John
  Brosio
1953–1972

Edward's Freezer
2501 Soquel Drive
Santa Cruz
1980s

El Azteca
1602 Mission Street
Santa Cruz
Jesus and Rosa Reyes
1980–1983
Mexican Cuisine

El Paisano Tamales
609 Beach Street and 611 Beach
  Street
Santa Cruz
Manuel and John Galan
1970–2012
Mexican Cuisine

El Rocco (Club)
605 Beach Street
Santa Cruz
Frank Battaglia and Sal T.
  Dinapoli
1948–1952
Italian Cuisine

Emi
1609 Cedar Street
Santa Cruz
Kyoung (Suki) Kang
1986–1996
Korean Fusion Cuisine

Facelli's
2830 West Cliff Drive
Santa Cruz
Louie M. and Eva J. Facelli
1959–1974

The Farm (The Greenhouse at)
5525 Soquel Drive
Soquel
Stephen Boysol
1976–1992

**Father Divine Peace
Restaurant**
401 Front Street
Santa Cruz
Nancy Roussel (dba Ann Sunlight)
1941–1942

Fino's Teahouse
9099 Soquel Drive
Aptos
Prem M. Rodriguez and Frances
B. Sharpe
1978–1979

Fjord's Smorgette
1549 Forty-First Avenue
Capitola
John L. Duran
1965–1976
Held bridge tournaments

Front Street Pub
516 Front Street
Santa Cruz
Gerry J. Turgeon
1985–2000

Garbini's Court and Tavern
3820 Soquel Drive
Santa Cruz
Art and Walt Garbini
1951–1965
Italian Cuisine

Gingerbread Boy
12135 Highway 9
Boulder Creek
Al and Bernice Louise Stafford
1970s
Specialty was lemon chicken

**Goebel and Suk's (Ship Ahoy,
The Ship)**
106 Beach Street and the Santa
Cruz Municipal Wharf
Santa Cruz
Joseph A. Goebel and Anton Suk
1943–1957

Gordon's Chuck House
191 Mt. Hermon Road
Scotts Valley
Don Gordon
1955–1970

Govinda's Natural Foods
1245 East Cliff Drive
Santa Cruz
1980s
Vegetarian Cuisine

Grapesteak
2621 Forty-First Avenue
Capitola
Jerry Neilsen
1967–1995

**Great American Wiener
Works**
1141 Soquel Avenue
Santa Cruz
Harold B. Cartright and Kay H.
James
1980s–1990s

The Greek
435 Front Street
Santa Cruz
1980s–1990s
Greek Cuisine

Harry's Surfrider
101 Main Street
Santa Cruz
Jerry Keefer, Harry and Josephine
    Lozinski, Loring H. Burns
1951–1967
"Home of the talking mynah bird"

**Heinz Biergarten Deli and
    Cafe**
1335 Pacific Avenue
Santa Cruz
Heinz and Joanna Gross
1978–1989 (destroyed in
    earthquake)
German Cuisine

High Street Local
224 Cardiff Place
Santa Cruz
Benn Westbrook
1971

Hi-Ho Eats
351 Ocean Street
Santa Cruz
Elmer Maupin; Florine K.
    Holman
1940s–1950s

Hoang Anh
2019 North Pacific Avenue
Santa Cruz
Lien Thi Tran
1986–1989
Vietnamese Cuisine

Hodgie's on the Boardwalk
Across from the Merry-go-Round
Santa Cruz Beach Boardwalk
    Concessionaire
Santa Cruz
Howard and Barbara Wetzel
1970s–1980s

**Hotel Palomar Coffee Shop
    and Cocktail Lounge**
125 Pacific Avenue
Santa Cruz
Various owners
1930–1989 (destroyed in
    earthquake)

**Hugo's Armenian Deli and
    Restaurant**
2332 Mission Street
Santa Cruz
Hugo R. and Nyla K. Naroyan;
    Dianne Erwood
1975–1979
Armenian Cuisine

**Il Trovatore Hotel, Dining
    Room and Cocktail Lounge**
124 Pacific Avenue and Beach
    Street
Santa Cruz
Peter and Ceasar E. Tori
1921–1961
Italian Cuisine
"Facing the Bay"

Impossible Restaurant
1226 Soquel Avenue
Santa Cruz
Gisele and Raymond Boulerice
1968–1979

Inaka
13375 Highway 9
Boulder Creek
1970s
Japanese Cuisine

India Joze
1001 Center Street
Santa Cruz
Jozseph Schultz
1972–1999
World Cuisine

It Fountain
1471 Freedom Boulevard
Watsonville
1950s

Jay's
Ocean Street and Water Street
Santa Cruz
Jay and Nancy Karr Sharmer
1970–1973

Karousel Drive-In
107 Ocean Street
Santa Cruz
1960s

Kim's
21401 East Cliff Drive and
  Fourteenth Avenue
Santa Cruz
Leon Lee
1960s–1970s
Chinese Cuisine

La Chaumiere
1314 Ocean Street
Santa Cruz
Ronald R. Madeira; Jean Claude
  Dufour
1975–1984
French Cuisine
"Building a reputation, not resting
  on one"

La Fogata
833 Front Street
Santa Cruz
1979–1989
Mexican Cuisine
"Featuring the music of El
  Mariachi Mixtlan"

La Manzana
100 West Lake Avenue
Watsonville
Alice, Manuel and Leonard
  Santana
1983–1985
Mexican Cuisine

**La Paloma Cafe and Cocktail
  Lounge**
6 Bulkhead Street
Santa Cruz
Alfonso Pieracci and G. Jerry
  Guazzini
1938–1946
Italian Cuisine

Locatelli's Inn
13300 Big Basin Way
Boulder Creek
Joe and Catherine Locatelli
1915–1955

Lorcne's Packing Shed
972 Main Street
Watsonville
1970s–1980s

The Lost Weekend
10 Pine Flat Road
Bonny Doon
Various owners
1920s–1980s

Louie's Place Cafe and Hotel Antonelli
29 Front Street
Santa Cruz
Louie Cantoni
1940–1943
Italian Cuisine
"The Bright Spot Day or Night"

L'Oustalou
118 Locust Street
Santa Cruz
Suzanne Grelson Rom
1973–1985
Mediterranean Cuisine

Lucca Lunch
28 Cooper Street
Santa Cruz
Joe Stefani and G. Antonetti
1940s
Italian Cuisine

Lunch Bowl
25 Third Street
Watsonville
1950s
Next door to the Cabrillo Lanes Bowling Alley

Mainsail Restaurant and Bar
175 West Cliff Drive
Santa Cruz
Chef William Prime
1999–2008
Inside the Dream Inn in Santa Cruz

Malio's on the Wharf
Center of the Santa Cruz Municipal Wharf
Santa Cruz
Malio J. Stagnaro
1965–1978

Manoff's Rancho Burger
139 Water Street
Santa Cruz
Thomas and Kathy Manoff
1959–2001

Mary's Tamale Parlor
1047 Freedom Boulevard
Watsonville
Zuniga Family
1950s–1980s
Mexican Cuisine

Maximilliano's
110 Cooper Street
Santa Cruz
Max Walden
1970s

Melvin's Pharmacy and Fountain
1415 Pacific Avenue
Santa Cruz
Melvin McRae, owner; Art Weybright, pharmacist
1925–1974

Micossi's Venetian Inn
1296 West Cliff Drive
Santa Cruz
Frank Micossi, manager; Rose
 Micossi, chef
1940–1957
Italian Cuisine

Mike's Soul Food
139 Water Street
Santa Cruz
Mike Mitchell
Chef DJ Marc Peterson
2001–2004
Soul Food

Miramar Bar and Grill
Main Street
Watsonville
Nick and Katie Derpich, George
 Lucich, Pete Derpich and
 Clement Ivelich
1947–1998

Miramar Fish Grotto
Center of the Municipal Wharf
Santa Cruz
Mary P. Carniglia; Parma
 Marcenaro and Patty Ghio;
 Charles F. and Charles Jr.
 Marcenaro
1941–2015

Mon Desir Dining Inn
Old Santa Cruz Watsonville Highway
 (one mile south of Rio Del Mar)
Aptos
Peter and Anna Beatrice Caplette;
 Alex Tummers; Edna and Ray
 Messini
1957–1964

Moscatelli's
4150 Capitola Road
Capitola
Raymond Le Doux and Herbert
 Cropper; Robert Latshaw and
 Jack Lyon
1979–1982

"Mother" Brown's Soul Food
231 Wilkes Circle
Santa Cruz
Vester "Mother" Brown
1970–1980
Soul Food

Nature's Harvest Natural Foods Restaurant
2-2145 East Cliff Drive
Santa Cruz
Marion D. Wieland
1970s
Vegetarian Cuisine

New Davenport Cash Store
1 Davenport Avenue
Davenport
Bruce and Marcia McDougal
1977–1987

New Riverside
210 Barson Street
Santa Cruz
K.M. Chan
Chef Lou Hai Yuen; Manager
 Francis Tong
1973–1984
Chinese Cuisine

Old Theatre Cafe
106 Walnut Avenue
Santa Cruz
Lorenz and Thea M. Rothbucher
1977–1994

Olivard's at the Wharf
West entrance of the Santa Cruz
    Municipal Wharf
Santa Cruz
Joe Olivieri and Tommy Edwards;
    J.L. Olivieri and Angelo W. Rossi
1946–1961
After a disastrous fire, the
    redwood building was
    completely torn down

The Palm Court
125 Pacific Avenue, in the St.
    George Hotel
Santa Cruz
Andy Balich, hotel's owner
1929–1989 (destroyed in
    earthquake)

Pan's
303 Potrero Street #5, in the Old
    Sash Mill
Santa Cruz
Nicolas A. Kneen
1970s–1980s

Pasatiempo Inn
555 Highway 17
Santa Cruz
1962–1987

Peachwood's Grill and Bar
555 Highway 17
Santa Cruz
1962–1987

Pearl Alley Bistro
110 Pearl Alley (upstairs)
Santa Cruz
Odette Emery, Marilyn and Eric
    Strayer; Marc Westberg and
    Mark Curtis
1973–2007

Pep Creameries Ltd.
1201 Pacific Avenue
Santa Cruz
1950s

Persimmon House
3010 North Main Street
Soquel
Robert Engler and Yuriko Hayashi
1978–1991
Japanese Cuisine

Pete's Family Restaurant
2018 Mission Street
Santa Cruz
Demetri J. and Panayotis Gouskos;
    Todd Todd
1980s–1999

Philippine Gardens Cafe
200 Main Street
Watsonville
Rosita Tabasa-Estrada
1938–1989
Filipino Cuisine

Piroska's
4720 Soquel Drive
Soquel
Margit and Bill Inanchy
1980s
Hungarian Cuisine

The Plaza Bakery
1550 Pacific Avenue
Santa Cruz
Mario, Eleanor and Eugene
    Tartaglino
1924–1989 (destroyed in
    earthquake)

Pogonip Lodge Clubhouse
333 Golf Club Drive
Santa Cruz
1912–1986
Refreshments were served in both
    the clubroom and outdoors, with
    special dinners for members and
    guests of the Casa del Rey Golf
    and Club Links and Polo Fields

**Polivio's Restaurant and
    Back Door**
21515 East Cliff Drive
Santa Cruz
Astrid and Paul Makris
1970–2001
Famous for its karaoke nights

Pontiac Grill
429 Front Street
Santa Cruz
George Ow, Larry Chew and
    Catherine Daniels
1986–2002

Portola House
3326 Portola Drive
Santa Cruz
Tony Ziro and Paul Gallus
1976–2007

Positively Front Street
44 Front Street and then 516 Front
    Street
Santa Cruz
Barry Jones and Lou Meadows
1970s–2004

Primitzia, Trattoria
502 Bay Avenue
Capitola
Catherine Faris
1985–1989
Italian Cuisine

Pronto Pup Drive-In
611 Main Street
Watsonville
Dick and Lurine Crocker
1950s

Ranjeet's
3051 Porter Street
Soquel
Ranjeet Lal
1980s

**Resetar Banquet Room and
    Coffee Shop**
15 West Lake Avenue
Watsonville
Joe Batich
1927–1990
The five-story building designed by
    William H. Weeks was damaged
    in the 1989 earthquake

Rice Bowl Cafe
275 Pacific Avenue
Santa Cruz
William Jung, Ramond Fong and
    Lillian Lowe
Tea Cup's Dan Y. Lee was
    manager in 1941
1938–1943
Mandarin Cuisine

Rick's Burger Pit
1820 Mission Street
Santa Cruz
Ricketts family
1961–1973

Right Livelihood Pizza
1721 Mission Street
Santa Cruz
Frederic Luskin and Patty Toback
1979–Early 1980s
Vegetarian, whole wheat pizza

River and Fern
901 River Street
Randall and Patricia Jacobsen
1980s
Featured Cornish pasties and
    shepherd pies

**The Riverside Hotel and
    Restaurant**
210 Barson Street
Santa Cruz
Pete Marchese, Larry Moise and
    Jack Genovesi
1948–1972

**The Riviera Restaurant and
    Hotel**
144 Pacific Avenue
Santa Cruz
Mary P. Carniglia
1945–1959
Italian Cuisine

Ron-De-Voo Restaurant
Corner of Mill and Main Streets
Ben Lomond
Lou Galetta
1940s–1970s

**Roudell's Restaurant and
    Coffee Shop**
1349 Pacific Avenue
Santa Cruz
Art Mason and Jack Rohan
1948–1957

Royal Grill
414 Main Street
Watsonville
Nick Derpich, George Lucich and
    Clement Ivelich
1940s

Ruth's Hamburgers
Entrance 3 of the Boardwalk
Santa Cruz Beach Boardwalk
    Concessionaire
Santa Cruz
Ruth and Glenn Hunter; Victor
    Marini Jr.
1938–1970s

Sāba Club and Caribbean Ballroom
110 Monterey Avenue
Capitola
Jack and Brad Macdonald
1954–1957

Saddle Rock Cafe and Coffee Shop
67 Pacific Avenue (inside the St. George Hotel)
Geo. J. Carstulovich, manager
1938–1989 (destroyed in earthquake)

Salmon Poacher
3035 North Main Street
Soquel
Howard Philippi; John Smith
1976–1980s

Santa Cruz Hotel
1003 Cedar Street
Santa Cruz
Stella Pera; John Righetti, Louie Facelli and Don Stefani; George H. Goebel and Anton Suk; Al Castagnola, Friend (Amigo) Arevalo and Annie Righetti; Frank Cardinale; (various business partnerships)
1928–1990
Italian Cuisine

Santa Cruz Hotel Bar & Grille
1003 Cedar Street (upstairs)
Santa Cruz
1976–1993

Seafood Mama's
820 Bay Avenue
Capitola
Ted and Pat Durkee
1980–1989
One of the hosts for the Dixieland Jamboree in Capitola

Seychelle's
313 Cedar Street
Santa Cruz
Cindy Lepore-Hart
1978–1991
Italian Cuisine

Ship Ahoy (The Ship)
106 Beach Street and the Santa Cruz Municipal Wharf
Geo. H. Goebel and Anton Suk; J.L. Olivieri and Angelo Rossi
1944–1957

Sloppy Joe's
118 Riverside
Santa Cruz
Frank and Peggy Saporito
1940s–1950s
Advertised no alcohol and pickled pig's feet; sawdust on floor

Spivey's 5-Spot Drive-In
400 Water Street
Santa Cruz
Thomas S. Spivey
1950s–1960s

Steffanetti's
167 Pacific Avenue
Santa Cruz
Don Stefani and Giuseppe
  Antonetti
1944–1946
Held a contest to come up with
  the name and offered a ten-
  dollar prize

St. Francis Grill
Beach and Cliff Streets
Santa Cruz
Peter Pappas
1907–1940s

St. George Hotel
Many restaurants and cafes over
  the years
67 Pacific Avenue
Santa Cruz
Frederick C. Hotaling, owner and
  builder; Geo. J. Carstulovich and
  Amigo Arevalo, managers
1897–1989 (destroyed in
  earthquake)

Sticky Wicket
217 Cathcart Street, Santa Cruz,
  then moved to 2535 Mar Vista
  Drive, Aptos
Vic and Sidney Jowers
1959–1964

Stubendorff Tamale Parlor
1013 River Street
Santa Cruz
Albert P., Ora and Vernon
  Stubendorff
1925–1956

Suzanne's By the Sea
427 Capitola Avenue
Capitola
Suzanne Pagni
1970s–1980s
Spanish Cuisine with an oyster bar
  upstairs

The Swan (Heavenly Goose)
1538 Pacific Avenue
Santa Cruz
Sue G. Granger-Akin
1977–1989 (destroyed in earthquake)
Chinese Cuisine

Swiss American Hotel
24–27 Water Street
Santa Cruz
Quirico "Zep" and Guido
  Borradori
1920s–1948
Swiss and Italian Cuisine
Survived the years of Prohibition

Tampico Kitchen and Lounge
Started across from the Boardwalk,
  then moved to 822 Pacific
  Avenue
Santa Cruz
Julio and Otila Gomez
1955–2016
Mexican Cuisine

Tapu's Breakfast Hut
1116 Soquel Avenue
Santa Cruz
Frank I. Frietas (dba Iopa Tapu)
1975–1991
Owner was famous for performing
  Samoan knife and fire dances

Tea Cup Restaurant
1538½ Pacific Avenue
Santa Cruz
Dan Y. and Rose Yee; Don J. Yee
1946–1989 (destroyed in
    earthquake)
Chinese Cuisine

Theo's
3101 North Main Street
Soquel
Greta and Ethan Hamm
1980s

**Thunder Trading and
    Frontier Deli, Slightly
    Kosher Irving's**
1134 Soquel Avenue
Santa Cruz
Lynne and Charles Gill
1978–1989
Jewish Deli and Kosher Cuisine

**Tip Top Coffee Shop and
    Diner**
2403 Mission Street
Santa Cruz
Mary Alice Tarbell; Bobbie and
    Earl Duntley; Jim E. Guerreiro
1958–1990
For a brief period in the 1970s, it
    served Bavarian cuisine

Trout Farm Inn
7701 East Zayante Road
Felton
Bill Fischer; Bob Follmar
Started in 1946

Turteen
Seventeenth Avenue and Portola
    Drive
Santa Cruz
1960s

Twelve Winds
175 West Cliff Drive (in the Dream
    Inn)
Santa Cruz
Chef Robert Canepa; Chef
    William Prime
1964–2000s

**Twenty-Five, Twenty-Five
    (2525)**
2525 Main Street
Soquel
Eli Bariteau and Frank Leal
1979–1991

Victorian Oak House
230 Mt. Hermon Road, Kings
    Village Shopping Center
Scotts Valley
Garth McDonald
1980s

The Western
2380 Portola Drive
Santa Cruz
Tony G. Darwish
1960s

**White House Creamery,
    Fountain Service**
385 Soquel Avenue
Santa Cruz
Joseph and Myrne Lytle
1940s

Whole Earth Restaurant
Redwood Tower building at
  University of California, Santa
  Cruz
Santa Cruz
Dr. Paul A. Lee, Jerry Lasko, Herb
  Schmidt
Chef Sharon Cadwallader
1970–2002

**Wild Goose Restaurant and
  Saloon**
100 Main Street
Ben Lomond
Mike Johns
1970s

Wild Thyme Cafe
110 Cooper Street (downstairs)
Santa Cruz
Dr. Paul A. and Charlene Lee
Chef Joanne Le Boeuf
1974

Woolworth's Luncheonette
1213 Pacific Avenue
Santa Cruz
1956–1997

**Ye Old Danish Inn, The Stork
  Inn**
Corner of Scotts Valley Drive and
  Hacienda Drive
Scotts Valley
Harold Hauge
1952–1965
Danish Smorgasbord

Ye Olde Dutch Inn
Corner of Scotts Valley Drive and
  Hacienda Drive
Scotts Valley
Homer L. Graver; Ralph and
  Mabel Blaylock; Harold Chivers
1941–1952

Zanze's Rocky Falls
Los Gatos Highway (off of
  Highway 17, now the Moose
  Lodge)
Santa Cruz
Louie Zanze
1949–1960

Zanzibar
2332 Mission Street
Santa Cruz
Phillip Saad
1980s
Polynesian Cuisine

Zorba the Buddha
538 Seabright Avenue
Santa Cruz
Operated by the followers of
  Bhagwan Rajneesh
1980s
Vegetarian Cuisine

Zunigas's
100 Aviation Way
Watsonville
John, Angela and Ed Zuniga
1980s–2011

Bibliography

Interviewees

Ashelman, Martha Work
Bargetto, John
Bariteau, Barry
Beauregard, Jim
Bottoms, Rita
Brown, Sara
Burke, Ted
Castagnola, Jill
Champion, Carol
Chyle, Renee
Dolgenos, Peggy
Durant, Jessie
Evans, Lori
Facelli, Melinda
Faris, Catherine
Ferry, Mike
Flocchini, John
Flocchini, Rich
Fontana, Taylor
George, Bert
Gizdich, Nita

Hall, Joe
Heebner, Geri Derpich
Hosmer, Nani
Hosmer, Steve
Hunter, Jermaine
Imperio, Sandi
Kirchner, Carol
Klempnauer, Len
Kubas, Carmen
Leask, Sam
Le Boeuf, Joanne
Lee, Charlene
Lee, Dr. Paul A.
Lepore-Hart, Cindy
Manfre, Gary
Manoff, Kathleen
Manoff, Tom
McCarthy, Ellen
McDougal, Bruce
McDougal, Marcia
McKoy, Tom
McLean, Allan

McPherson, Bruce
Michalak, Joe
Murphy, Mary
Nama, Jeremy
Novo, Marla
Page, Linda
Page, Steve
Peterson, DJ Marc
Pokriots, Marion Dale
Poulos, Virginia
Prara, Sierra
Prime, Bill
Prime, Fiona
Reyes, Paulino
Rom, Suzanne Grelson
Santana, Leonard
Schmidt, Marisa
Schultz, Jozseph
Sharmer, Nancy Karr
Sharp, Melody
Stagnaro, Dino
Stagnaro, Malio

Stefani, Leo
Swift, Carolyn
Tara, John
Tupper, Jerri
Turgeon, Gerry

Van Valkenberg, Ned
Waters, Christina
Watson, Sharon
Nystrom
Watson-Wolf, Jennifer

Weybright, Art
Weybright, Dee
Whiting, Jeanne
Wilshusen, Linda

Books

Bargetto, John E., and Geoffrey Dunn. *Vintage Bargetto: Celebrating a Century of California Winemaking*. Soquel, CA: Self-published, 2013.

Beal, Chandra, and Richard Beal. *Santa Cruz Beach Boardwalk: The Early Years, Never a Dull Moment*. Aptos, CA: The Pacific Group, 2003.

Bergeron, Victor. *Trader Vic's Helluva Man's Cookbook*. New York: Doubleday, 1976.

Braden, Donna R. *Leisure and Entertainment in America*. Detroit: Wayne State University, 1988.

Cadwallader, Sharon, and Judi Ohr. *Whole Earth Cook Book: Access to Natural Cooking*. Preface by Paul Lee. Boston: Houghton Mifflin, 1972.

Chase, John Leighton. *The Sidewalk Companion to Santa Cruz Architecture*. 3rd ed. Edited by Judy Steen. Santa Cruz: MAH, 2005.

Clark, Dave, and Gus Gregory. *Reflections of the Santa Cruz Harbor: A Portal to Monterey Bay*. Santa Cruz: Self-published, 2005.

Comelli, Ivano Franco. *La Nostra Costa (Our Coast). A Family's Journey to and from the North Coast of Santa Cruz, California (1923–1983)*. Bloomington, IN: Author House, 2006.

Croft, Virginia. *Recycled as Restaurants: Case Studies in Adaptive Reuse*. New York: Whitney Library of Design, 1991.

Fogelson, George J. *Between the Redwoods and the Bay. The Jewish Community of Santa Cruz County, California from the Gold Rush to the Twenty-First Century*. Santa Cruz: MAH, 2017.

Forstall, Richard L., ed. *Population of Counties by Decennial Census: 1900 to 1990*. Washington, D.C.: U.S. Bureau of the Census, Population Division, 1995.

Gee, Bonnie, ed. *A Taste of Santa Cruz: Recipes from Restaurants and Farms of Santa Cruz County*. Santa Cruz: Environmental Council, 1980.

Hemp, Michael Kenneth. *Cannery Row: The History of Old Ocean View Avenue*. Monterey, CA: The History Company, 1986.

Hines, Duncan. *Adventures in Good Eating: Good Eating Along the Highways of America*. Bowling Green, KY: Adventures in Good Eating, Inc., 1944.

Izzo, Joseph, Jr., Douglas Kincaid and Joseph Mangelli. *A Forkful of San Jose and the South Bay*. 2nd ed. San Jose, CA: Izkinelli, 1977.

Jones, Donna, ed. *Santa Cruz County: A Century*. Santa Cruz: Santa Cruz Sentinel, 1999.

Kerry, Katherine. *Look What's Cooking! In and Near San Francisco*. San Francisco: Filmer Bros., 1951.

Koch, Margaret. *The Walk Around Santa Cruz Book: A Look at the City's Architectural Treasures*. Fresno, CA: Valley Publishing, 1978.

Lawson, Lois Ackerman. *Growing Up in Santa Cruz*. Santa Cruz: CruzBrand, 2015.

Lee, Dr. Paul A. *There Is a Garden in the Mind: A Memoir of Alan Chadwick and the Organic Movement in California*. Berkeley, CA: North Atlantic Books, 2013.

Lingeman, Richard R. *Don't You Know There's a War On? The American Homefront 1941–1945*. New York: Putnam's, 1972.

May, Antoinette. *Haunted Houses of California: A Ghostly Guide to Haunted Houses and Wandering Spirits*. 2nd ed. San Carlos, CA: Wide World, 2002.

McLean, Hulda Hoover. *Almost a Hundred Years*. Santa Cruz: Waddell Creek Association, 2002.

Mekis, Donna F., and Kathryn Mekis Miller. *Blossoms into Gold, The Croatians in the Pajaro Valley*. Capitola, CA: Capitola Book Co., 2009.

Miss California Pageant Programs. 1954, 1958, 1969 and 1979.

Nelson, Robert L. *Remembering Our Own: The Santa Cruz County Military Roll of Honor 1861–2010*. Santa Cruz: Otter B. Books, 2010.

O'Hare, Sheila, and Irene Berry. *Santa Cruz, California*. Charleston, SC: Arcadia Publishing, 2003.

Paizis, Suzanne. *The Joaquin Castro Adobe in the Twenty-First Century, from Earthquake to Earthquake*. Santa Cruz: Otter B. Books, 2002.

Phillips, Jim. *Surf, Skate & Rock Art of Jim Phillips*. Atglen, PA: Schiffer, 2004.

Pokriots, Marion Dale. *Remembering Scotts Valley*. Santa Cruz: Norman Poitevin, 2007.

Polk's Directories. Santa Cruz County, 1940–1989.

Rowland, Leon. *Santa Cruz, The Early Years*. Santa Cruz: Paper Vision Press, 1980.

Santa Cruz Seaside Company, The. *The Santa Cruz Beach Boardwalk: A Century by the Sea*. Berkeley, CA: Ten Speed Press, 2007.

Scofield, W.L. *California Fishing Ports*. N.p.: State of California Department of Fish and Game, 1954.

Seapy, Dr. Donald E. *Scotts Valley: As It Was and As It Would Become*. Scotts Valley, CA: Published by author, 2001.

Staff of the *Santa Cruz Sentinel*. *5:04 p.m. The Great Quake of 1989: A Pictorial of the Devastation in Santa Cruz County*. 2nd ed. Santa Cruz: *Santa Cruz Sentinel*, 1989.

Swift, Carolyn. *By-the-Sea: A History of the Capitola Begonia Festival.* Capitola, CA: Capitola Begonia Festival, 1992.

Thomas, Jerry. *The bar-tenders guide: a complete cyclopedia of plain and fancy drinks; containing clear and reliable directions for mixing all the beverages used in the United States.* New York: Dick and Fitzgerald, 1862.

Tiano, Jack. *The American Bartenders School Guide to Drinks.* New York: Rutledge, 1981.

Tiffen, Richard, Pat Pfremmer and the Ladies of Bonny Doon Club. *Memories of the Mountain: Family Life in Bonny Doon (1800–2000).* Bloomington, IN: AuthorHouse, 2004.

van Zuiden, Gordon, and Carolyn Swift. *The Grand Hotel Capitola.* 2nd ed. Capitola, CA: Capitola Historical Museum, 2007.

Articles

California State Military Museum. "Administrative History of U.S. Naval Special Hospital, Santa Cruz, California, June 30, 1946." History Library at the U.S. Navy Bureau of Medicine and Surgery ("BuMed").

Hibble, John. "This Old House." Aptos History Museum, July 2015. Research article done on the history of the property and its owners at 9051 Soquel Boulevard; starting as a house, a retirement home and its commercial use as a restaurant including The Charles Dickens and Chez Renee.

Office of Institutional Research, Assessment and Policy Studies. "Historical Enrollment by Student Level and Quarter, since 1966." UCSC Data Warehouse, May 8, 2018.

Resolution No. NS-15, 026. A Resolution of the City Council of the City of Santa Cruz Supporting the "Can and Bottle Recycling Initiative" (1982).

Steen, Judy. "The Lost Weekend." Research for the Santa Cruz Museum of Art and History (MAH) Historic Landmark Blue Plaque Awards. Compiled in 2011.

Magazines

Bingham, Barbara J. "Ration Books." *Antiques Journal* (Dubuque, IA) 30, no. 3 (March 1975).

Hellman, Geoffrey T. "The Talk of the Town." *New Yorker,* July 18, 1964.

Holiday: An entire issue devoted to San Francisco (Philadelphia) 29, no. 4 (April 1961). Contains Herb Caen's seven-page article "Handbook of San Francisco's Restaurants," which features Victor Bergeron's Trader Vic's.

Howard, J. "The 'Non-Drinker' as an Ally." *Bartender* (Vero Beach, FL) 7, no. 3 (July 1986).
Spiegel Catalog (Chicago). "Restaurant Equipment." 1943.

Websites

California Food Handler Card Law. "SB 602/SB (2010), SB 303 (2011)." Santa Cruz. www.co.santa-cruz.ca.us/eh/ehhome.htm.
Dixon, Vince. "Heaven Was a Place in Harlem." Eater. Published October 29, 2018. www.eater.com/a/father-divine.
Jarrell, Randall. "Malio J. Stagnaro: The Santa Cruz Genovese. Interviewed and Edited by Elizabeth Spedding Calciano." Permalink Authors Regional History Project, UCSC Library. June 1, 1975. https://escholarship.org/uc/item/79d536j6
Labor Code 6404.5 of 1995. "The California Legislature finds and declares that regulation of smoking in the workplace is a matter of statewide interest and concern." California Air Resources Board. https://ww3.arb.ca.gov/toxics/ets/workplace_smoking.pdf.

Libraries

Santa Cruz Public Library
Watsonville Public Library

Museums and Historical Associations

Aptos History Museum
Capitola Historical Museum
Dallas Historical Society
Pajaro Valley Historical Association
Santa Cruz Museum of Art and History (MAH)

Newspapers

California Digital Newspaper Collection (https://cdnc.ucr.edu)
Santa Cruz Sentinel

Index

T

"Tequila Sunrise," 1973 song 110
Trader Vic's 27, 38

U

UCSC 50, 64, 70, 73, 78, 88, 91,
    124
"Under the Boardwalk," 1964 song
    52
Union Ice Company 120

W

Walden, Max 76, 78
Watsonville 32, 35, 41, 62, 66, 96,
    100
Watsonville Coast Produce 104,
    121, 124
Woodies on the Wharf 101
Work, Geraldine G. 16
World War II 9, 15, 18, 26, 29, 35,
    48, 74, 97, 102, 121, 125, 129
Wrigley's Chewing Gum
    Manufactory 52

About the Author

Liz Pollock first came to Santa Cruz in 1975 to visit some friends at the University of California, Santa Cruz campus for the Valentine's Day Waltz at Cowell College. In the large dining hall, students and guests waltzed with professors to live chamber music. Liz loved walking along West Cliff Drive with her friends and then eating a delicious Italian dinner on the Santa Cruz Wharf. As soon as she could, she transferred from California State, Los Angeles to UCSC, where she majored in comparative literature and worked in the cafeteria to help make ends meet. After college, Liz went to the American Bartenders School in San Jose and learned to be a Certified Mixologist. She was hired at Adolph's Italian Family Style Restaurant as their first female bartender and worked a combination of day and night shifts from 1985 to 1990. Liz met her husband there and made many good friends.

Liz has owned the Cook's Bookcase since 2007; it specializes in unique books and ephemera on cookery and wine. She is a member of The Book

A photograph of the author that was taken after a busy night at Adolph's Italian Family Restaurant in 1985. *Author's collection.*

Club of California, The Independent Online Booksellers Association (IOBA), The Northern California Independent Booksellers Association (NCIBA), Slow Food USA, The Agricultural History Project, Pasadena Heritage, Santa Cruz County Chamber of Commerce, Pajaro Valley Chamber of Commerce and Agriculture and The James Beard Foundation. Liz and her family live in a restored 1914 California Craftsman Bungalow in the beautiful coastal town of Santa Cruz.